FIRESIDE

HOME OWNER'S WORKSHOP

William K. Ermeling

FIRESIDE

A Fireside Book Published by Simon and Schuster

Copyright © 1977 by Home Owner's Way, Inc.
A Fireside Book
Published by Simon and Schuster
A Division of Gulf & Western Corporation
Simon & Schuster Building
Rockefeller Center
1230 Avenue of the Americas
New York, New York 10020

Manufactured in the United States of America

1   2   3   4   5   6   7   8   9   10

Library of Congress Cataloging in Publication Data

Ermeling, William K
Home owner's workshop.

(A Fireside book)
Includes index.
1.   Dwellings–Maintenance and repair–Amateurs'
manuals. 2.   Carpentry–Amateurs' manuals.   I.   Title.
TH4817.3.E75   1977   694'.6   76-57216
ISBN 0-671-22634-7

Contents

HOW™
HOME OWNER'S WAY, inc.

HOME OWNER'S WORKSHOP

How to use this book and save!

Owning your own home is nice and it is usually a good hedge against inflation. However, maintenance and repair costs are spiraling upward. As a homeowner, you can save a great deal of money by doing more things for yourself ... and you can with the help of this book!

You won't have any difficulty understanding the illustrated step-by-step procedures or the language because it has been written by a homeowner FOR homeowners. I would like to make a few suggestions for getting the most value from the book.

1. After reviewing the contents, thumb through each page ... this will help you get an understanding of how it is laid out for your convenience and easy reference.

2. When undertaking a job, read everything that relates to it FIRST. You will then recognize how each step leads into the next ... while being forewarned of adjustments or changes which may be necessary "on the job."

3. Even if your plans only relate to hanging bookshelves or repairing a wall surface, take the time to read about basic wall construction. It can make the job easier ... in some cases, keep you out of trouble.

The last portion of the book deals with specific projects ... some minor in nature; others, dealing with building projects such as basement recreation rooms, attic bedrooms and the conversion of a garage area into a family room.

You will find this book completely useful because it will help you think through the project, prepare for each step including material ordering and then give you the step-by-step guides for getting the job done.

Doing things for yourself can be constructive, therapeutic ... and fun. The money you save will be all yours!

TOOLS

BASIC HANDYMAN'S KIT

HAMMER - 16 oz. curved claw common or nail hammer with wood, solid or tubular steel or fiberglass handle. Second hammer 13 oz. Head should be drop forged for hardness and firmly attached to handle. Find a hammer that feels good to you!

SCREWDRIVERS - Small and medium sizes of both regular and Phillips head. Handle may be wood or plastic but should not have sharp edges that can cut into the hand. Use insulated screwdrivers for electrical work.

COMBINATION PLIERS - Also called common or slip joint pliers. Should be drop forged with deep teeth for gripping ability. Six and eight inch most popular size.

UTILITY KNIFE - All purpose knife with replaceable blades. May have fixed or retractable (best) blade. Blade should be firmly held in place.

HAND SAW - 24" or 26" crosscut or combination saw with 8 to 10 teeth per inch. Should have rust-resistant tempered spring or stainless steel blade. Handle may be wood, plastic or metal.

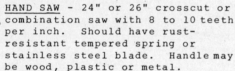

SABRE SAW - Most versatile and easily operated power saw available. Although it cuts slower than other power saws, if the proper type and length of blade are used, it will saw almost any material. Should be 2 speed or variable speed of at least 1/5 hp. Also, one should have an assortment of 4 to 6 best quality wood and metal blades in order to meet most needs. Available for rough and finish cutting of wood, aluminum and other metals, plywood and paneling.

ELECTRIC DRILL - With attachments this tool has almost unlimited uses. Should be 3/8" variable speed. Reversing action optional.

DRILL BITS - Assortment of small high speed bits for both wood and metal. Use wood auger, flat spade or expansive bits for larger holes in wood.

MASONRY BIT - Used to drill holes in all kinds of masonry, 1/2" most often used size. Should have tungsten carbide tip.

PILOT BIT - Used to pre-drill holes for wood screws. Should have pilot bit for each size wood screw to be used.

EXTENSION CORD - For use with power tools. Should be 25' or 50' long and of heavy duty construction.

DROP LIGHT - Also called extension or trouble light. Should be U.L. approved and of heavy duty construction.

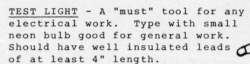

TEST LIGHT - A "must" tool for any electrical work. Type with small neon bulb good for general work. Should have well insulated leads of at least 4" length.

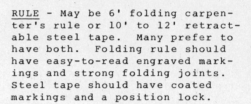

RULE - May be 6' folding carpenter's rule or 10' to 12' retractable steel tape. Many prefer to have both. Folding rule should have easy-to-read engraved markings and strong folding joints. Steel tape should have coated markings and a position lock.

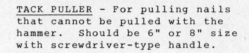

ADJUSTABLE WRENCH - 8" wrench with opening adjustable to at least 1" Should be drop forged and have adjustment lock. New type has slide rather than worm-screw adjustment.

TACK PULLER - For pulling nails that cannot be pulled with the hammer. Should be 6" or 8" size with screwdriver-type handle.

OIL CAN - Should be of 1/4 to 1/2 pint capacity with a 6" to 10" flexible spout. Keep filled with general purpose motor lubricating oil.

FLASHLIGHT - May be 2 to 5 cell regular, 6 volt or rechargeable. Keep spare bulb handy. Check batteries periodically for strength and leakage.

SAFETY GOGGLES - To be used with all power tools and with hand tools if there is any chance of flying splinters. Also use when working over head. Should be flexible enough for comfort while completely protecting the eyes.

OPTIONAL TOOLS FOR BASIC KIT

LEVEL - Wood or metal, 24" long. Should have replaceable vials (glass tubes). The bubble in the glass should be easily read.

STEEL SQUARE - Also called a framing square. A basic tool for marking with full set of tables. Can be used to measure stairs and rafters. Should be 18" x 24" with rust-resistant coating and should be very legibly marked.

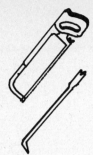

HACKSAW - Fine toothed saw used for cutting metal. Frame should be of sturdy construction and blade should have 24 teeth per inch for general purpose work.

PRY BAR - Used as a prying lever instead of a hammer or screwdriver for pulling large nails. Should be made of flat steel stock, tempered and 18" to 24" long.

FILES - One 6" and one 10" flat file. Should have single cut mill bastard cutting teeth for general use. Practical use ... sharpening garden tool edges.

WOOD CHISEL - One 1/4" and 1/2" width blade. Should have handle strong enough to allow light tapping with a hammer.

WIRE BRUSH - Should have handle and wire bristles firmly attached. Paint scraper optional.

GLASS CUTTER - Should have free rolling tungsten carbide cutting wheel. Store in plastic case to prevent damage to wheel.

TOOLS NICE TO HAVE

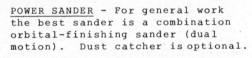

CIRCULAR SAW - Blade should be 6 1/2" or larger. Better quality circular saws have ball bearings and safety clutches. Use a combination blade for general work. Blades are available for almost everything, including metal and masonry.

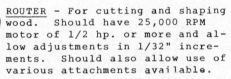

POWER SANDER - For general work the best sander is a combination orbital-finishing sander (dual motion). Dust catcher is optional.

ROUTER - For cutting and shaping wood. Should have 25,000 RPM motor of 1/2 hp. or more and allow adjustments in 1/32" increments. Should also allow use of various attachments available.

RADIAL ARM SAW - With attachments, can be a "one tool workshop." Should have at least an 8" blade, stops for 90°, 45° and 30° angle cuts and have attachments for other functions available.

UTILITY VISE - Should be table-mounted, with wide smooth jaws that will open at least 4". Adjustable angle base and changeable jaw plates optional.

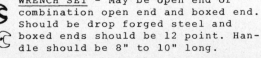

WRENCH SET - May be open end or combination open end and boxed end. Should be drop forged steel and boxed ends should be 12 point. Handle should be 8" to 10" long.

SAFETY TIPS FOR POWER TOOLS

1. KNOW YOUR POWER TOOL. Read the manual carefully; learn the tool's applications and limitations and its potential hazards.

2. GROUND ALL TOOLS--UNLESS DOUBLE INSULATED. If tool is equipped with 3-prong plug, it should be plugged into a 3-hold electrical receptacle. If adapter is used to accommodate 2-prong receptacle, the adapter wire must be attached to a KNOWN ground. NEVER remove third prong.

3. KEEP GUARDS IN PLACE and in working order.

4. KEEP WORK AREA CLEAN.

5. AVOID DANGEROUS ENVIRONMENT. Don't use power tool in damp or wet locations; keep work area well lit.

6. KEEP CHILDREN A SAFE DISTANCE AWAY.

7. STORE IDLE TOOLS. When not in use, tools should be stored in dry, high or locked-up place--out of reach of children.

8. DON'T FORCE TOOL. Do not exceed the rate for which it was designed.

9. USE RIGHT TOOL. Don't force small tool to do job of heavy-duty tool.

10. WEAR PROPER APPAREL. Avoid loose clothing, ties or jewelry that can get caught in moving parts. Use rubber gloves and footwear when working outside.

11. USE SAFETY GLASSES with most tools, also face or dust mask if cutting operation is dusty.

12. DON'T ABUSE CORD. Never carry tool by cord or yank it to disconnect. Keep cord from oil, heat and sharp edges.

13. SECURE WORK. Use clamps or vise to hold work; this frees both hands to operate tool.

14. DON'T OVERREACH. Keep proper footing and balance at all times.

15. MAINTAIN TOOLS WITH CARE. Keep sharp and clean, follow instructions for lubricating and changing accessories.

16. TURN OFF OR DISCONNECT TOOLS when not in use--before servicing, when changing attachments, etc. Turn off tool when talking to someone or when looking for something.

17. REMOVE ADJUSTING KEYS AND WRENCHES. Check that keys and adjusting wrenches are removed before turning tool on.

18. AVOID ACCIDENTAL STARTING. Don't carry plugged-in tool with finger on switch.

LEVER WRENCH PLIERS - Also called lock wrench pliers. Have a lever controlled vise for locking in place. Should be of drop forged steel and open to at least 1 1/4".

TONGUE AND GROOVE PLIERS - Allows adjustment to several jaw openings but will not slip into a larger jaw opening when in use. Ideal for extra leverage and gripping in tight places. Should be drop forged steel and 10" to 12" long.

HEXNUT DRIVE SET - Similar to screwdriver but used to drive small nuts in place of a wrench. Available as either fixed size or with interchangeable sockets. Fixed size best.

METAL SHEARS - Available in straight cut, combination and compound-leverage (aviation) types. Aviation type develops the greatest cutting leverage. Should be forged high carbon steel and heat-treated. Also available in left-handed and right-handed cut.

KEYHOLE SAW - Also called a wallboard or compass saw. Should have rust-resistant spring steel blade and a firmly attached handle.

STAPLE GUN - Not to be confused with the paper stapler. Has pistol grip squeeze handle and is used to "shoot" staples into wood. Should be of sturdy construction and allow use of several sizes of staples.

COLD CHISEL - Used to cut heavy metal. 1/2" wide, flat point style best for general use. Should be of high grade forged and tempered alloy steel.

NAIL SET - Used to drive finish nails slightly below nailing surface without marring surface. Should be of high grade forged and tempered alloy steel with slight **indentation on point to hold nail** when driving.

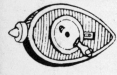

C-CLAMPS - General pupose clamp. Most useful size is 4" x 3". Should check to see that center screw stays in alignment with clamping surface.

CHALKLINE PLUMBLINE - Combination unit. Should have nylon cord and have cord lock. 50' to 100' length best for general use.

STUD DRIVER - Used to hold masonry nails when driving. Should have large safety flange at top and cushioned handle.

VOLT-OHM METER - Can be used in place of the test light and continuity tester and has ability to measure voltages, amp flow and resistance. Should be battery-type with several volt, amp and ohm scale ranges.

ALLEN WRENCHES - Complete set from 1/16" to 1/2". Should be high quality steel to prevent their bending or twisting out of shape in use.

SAWHORSE BRACKETS - Set of 4 brackets for 2 x 4's. Should be folding type of solid construction with holes for nailing to legs and cross piece.

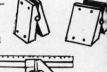

COMBINATION SQUARE - Used to mark lumber for 45 degree angle and square cuts. Should have locking 12" blade that stays in alignment in all blade settings.

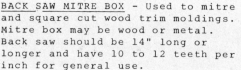

PLANE - 8" to 10" bench or smooth plane best for general use. Should have high grade tempered alloy steel blade with smooth bottom plate.

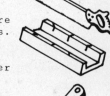

FINISH WORK TOOLS

BACK SAW MITRE BOX - Used to mitre and square cut wood trim moldings. Mitre box may be wood or metal. Back saw should be 14" long or longer and have 10 to 12 teeth per inch for general use.

JOINT KNIFE - Used to apply joint cement to drywall. Knife should be 4" to 6" wide and rust-resistant. A second knife 6" to 10" wide is sometimes used to apply finish coating of joint cement.

JOINT TROWEL - May be a plasterer's finishing trowel or taping-knife spreader, used to apply finish coat of joint cement. Should be 10" to 12" wide with a rust-resistant blade.

TILE NIPPERS - Not to be confused with end cutting nippers. The cutting edges of tile nippers do not quite come together when in closed position. Used to cut and shape ceramic tile. Should be drop forged and 6" to 8" long.

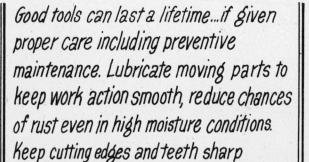

Good tools can last a lifetime...if given proper care including preventive maintenance. Lubricate moving parts to keep work action smooth, reduce chances of rust even in high moisture conditions. Keep cutting edges and teeth sharp and protected.

4

TOOLS CHECK LIST

HAVE	BASIC	WANT	HAVE	FINISH	WANT
✓	HAMMER		✓	MITRE BOX & BACK SAW	
✓	SCREWDRIVER		✓	JOINT KNIFE	
✓	COMBINATION PLIERS		✓	JOINT TROWEL	
✓	UTILITY KNIFE			TILE NIPPERS	
✓	HANDSAW				
✓	SABER SAW			NICE TO HAVE	
✓	SABER SAW BLADES		✓	CIRCULAR SAW	
✓	ELECTRICAL DRILL		✓	POWER SANDER	
✓	ELECTRICAL DRILL BITS			RADIAL ARM SAW	
	MASONRY BIT			ROUTER	
	PILOT BIT			UTILITY VISE	
✓	EXTENTION CORD		✓	WRENCH SET	
✓	DROP LIGHT			LEVER WRENCH PLIERS	
✓	TEST LIGHT			TONGUE & GROOVE PLIERS	
✓	STEEL RULE			HEXNUT DRIVE SET	
✓	CARPENTRY RULE			METAL SHEARS	
✓	ADJUSTABLE WRENCH			KEYHOLE SAW	
	TACK PULLER		✓	STAPLE GUN	
✓	OIL CAN		✓	STAPLES	
✓	FLASHLIGHT			COLD CHISEL	
✓	SAFETY GOGGLES		✓	C-CLAMPS	
				CHALKLINE/PLUMBLINE	
	OPTIONAL			STUD DRIVER	
✓	LEVEL			MASONRY NAILS	
✓	WIRE BRUSH		✓	ALLEN WRENCHES	
✓	STEEL SQUARE			NAIL SET	
✓	HACKSAW		✓	VOLT-OHM METER	
	GLASS CUTTER		✓	SAWHORSE BRACKETS	
	PRY BAR			PLANE	
✓	FILES			COMBINATION SQUARE	
✓	WOOD CHISELS				

USING AN ELECTRICAL TEST LIGHT

An electrical test light is more than a basic tool ... it is an important safety device. However, it should be tested in an outlet you know to be "live" to make certain the bulb is working and will glow when current is flowing.

To test a receptacle, one lead of the tester is slipped into each blade opening. The bulb will glow if the outlet is HOT! Switches are tested by placing a lead on each of the two screws holding the wire connections to the switch.

All 240-volt receptacles have 3-blade openings, the lower being the neutral or ground. Configurations differ according to the appliance being served. One lead is slipped into the neutral slot and the other into one of the hot line openings. This line is LIVE if the bulb glows. Be sure to check the other side of the 240 volt circuit ... leave the one test lead in the neutral slot and move the other to the untested slot. Each one carrys 120 V to make up the 240 V service.

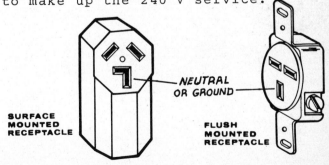

SURFACE MOUNTED RECEPTACLE

NEUTRAL OR GROUND

FLUSH MOUNTED RECEPTACLE

KNOW YOUR HOUSE

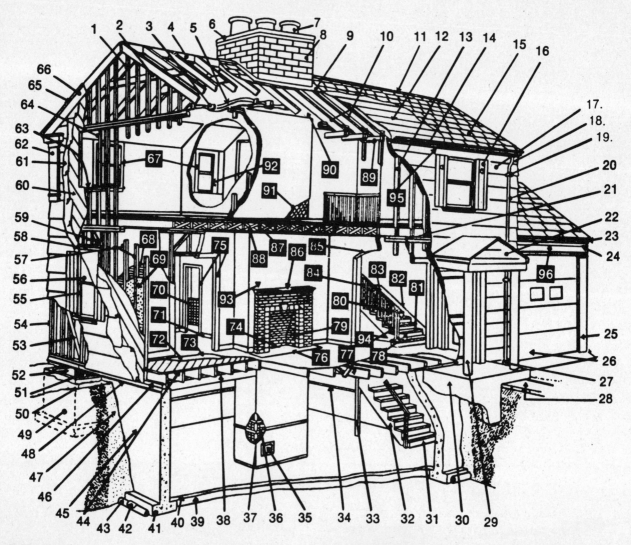

1. Gable Stud	25. Door Jamb	49. Window Well Wall	73. Finish Floor
2. Collar Beam	26. Garage Door	50. Grade Line	74. Ash Dump
3. Ceiling Joist	27. Downspout Shoe	51. Basement Sash	75. Door Trim-casing
4. Ridge Board	28. Sidewalk	52. Window Well	76. Fireplace Hearth
5. Insulation	29. Entrance Post	53. Corner Brace	77. Floor Joists
6. Chimney Cap	30. Entrance Platform	54. Corner Stud	78. Stair Riser
7. Chimney Flues	31. Stair Riser	55. Window Frame	79. Fire Brick
8. Chimney	32. Stair Stringer	56. Window Light	80. Newel Cap
9. Chimney Flashing	33. Girder Post	57. Wall Studs	81. Stair Tread
10. Rafters	34. Chair Rail	58. Header	82. Finish Stringer
11. Ridge	35. Cleanout Door	59. Window Cripple	83. Stair Rail
12. Roof Boards	36. Furring Strips	60. Wall Sheathing	84. Balusters
13. Stud	37. Corner Stud	61. Building Paper	85. Plaster Arch
14. Eave Gutter	38. Girder	62. Pilaster	86. Mantel
15. Roofing	39. Gravel Fill	63. Rough Header	87. Floor Joists
16. Blind or Shutter	40. Concrete Floor	64. Window Stud	88. Bridging
17. Bevel Siding	41. Foundation Footing	65. Cornice Moulding	89. Lookout
18. Downspout Gooseneck	42. Paper Strip	66. Fascia Board	90. Attic Space
19. Downspout Strap	43. Drain Tile	67. Window Casing	91. Metal Lath
20. Downspout Leader	44. Diagonal Subfloor	68. Lath	92. Window Sash
21. Double Plate	45. Foundation Wall	69. Insulation	93. Chimney Breast
22. Entrance Canopy	46. Sill Plate	70. Wainscoting	94. Newel
23. Garage Cornice	47. Backfill	71. Baseboard	95. Eave
24. Fascia	48. Termite Shield	72. Building Paper	96. Soffit

KNOW YOUR HOUSE
"FAMILIARITY BREEDS CONTENTMENT"

General

1. Outside Dimensions _____ Inside sq. ft. living space _____
2. Foundation: Poured concrete ____ Block ____ Stone ____ Other ____
3. Construction: Wood Frame ____ Brick ____ Brick Veneer ____ Stone or Block ____
   Other ____
4. Interior wall construction: Plaster ____ Drywall ____ Other ____
5. Approximate Age ____ Number of Rooms ____ Full Baths ____ Half Baths ____
6. Available Areas: Attic ____ Basement ____ Garage ____ Open Porch ____ Other ____

Plumbing

1. Water Supply Lines: Galvanized ____ Plastic ____ Copper ____
2. (a) Exact location of main entrance shut-off valve _____
   (b) Branch shut-off valves _____
   (c) Fixtures with shut-off valves or line stops _____
      Suggestion: Trace water lines. Tag hot and cold and the fixtures serviced.
3. Drain Lines: Lead ____ Galvanized ____ Cast Iron ____ Copper ____ Plastic ____
4. Location of tub, shower, etc., traps _____
   Suggestion: Label cleanouts and traps as to what fixture they drain.
5. (a) Location of main stack cleanout _____
   (b) Location of branch stack cleanouts _____
6. Water Heater: Gas ____ Electric ____
   Shut-off for (a) Gas Supply ____ (b) Electricity ____
   Locate and tag cold water supply valve.

Electrical

1. Exact location of entrance panel _____
2. Type: Fuse ____ Breaker ____ Amperes of service _____
3. Main electrical power shut-off (inside panel - main breaker or fuse ... outside
   panel - on-off lever or breaker switch) _____
4. Add-on panels: What appliance or circuit is served and how does it turn off -
   on-off lever, pull fuse or breaker switch? _____
5. Add-on panels: Shut-off method and what is served _____

Heating and Air Conditioning

1. (a) Type of heat: Gas ____ Oil ____ Coal ____ Electric ____
   (b) Forced Air ____ Gravity ____ Circulating Hot Water ____ Steam ____
   If gas ... location of main gas entrance valve (tag) _____
      Location of branch line valves (tag all gas lines and valves; identify the
      fixture each supplies _____
   If electric ... location of main or add-on panel on-off control _____
   Air conditioning main shut-off switch location _____
   Size and location of filter required (change at least every three months)
   _____
   Humidifier water line and shut-off valve location _____

Know your terms

ACOUSTICAL TILE - Special tile for walls and ceilings made of mineral, wood, vegetable fibers, cord or metal. Its purpose is to control sound volume while providing cover.

BALUSTERS - Upright supports of a hand rail.

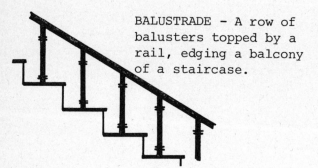

BALUSTRADE - A row of balusters topped by a rail, edging a balcony of a staircase.

BASEBOARD - A board along the floor against walls and partitions to hide gaps.

BATT - Insulation in the form of a blanket, rather than loose filling.

BATTEN - Small thin strips covering joints between wider boards on exterior building surfaces.

BEAM - One of the principal horizontal wood or steel members of a building.

BEARING WALL - Any wall that acts to support weight above as exterior walls support the roof system. Interior walls can be bearing if they support joists. Bearing walls utilize a double top plate.

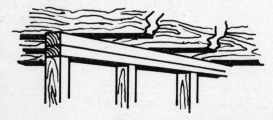

BRACE - A piece of wood or other material used to form a triangle and stiffen some part of a structure.

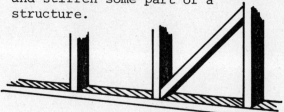

BRICK VENEER - Brick used as the outer surface of a framed wall.

BRIDGING - (Also called spacer blocks, cats or cross bracing.) Short cross members or bracing between studs or joists. Used to maintain alignment or support of a fixture or another member.

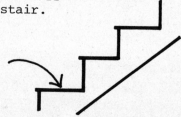

BUTT JOINT - Joining point of two pieces of wood or molding.

CARRIAGE - Notched member of stair framing which supports risers and treads of a stair.

CASEMENT - A window sash that opens on hinges of the vertical edge.

CASING - Door or window facing trim around jamb.

CHAIR RAIL - Wooden molding on a wall around a room at the level of a chair back.

CHASE - A groove in a masonry wall or through a floor to accommodate pipes or ducts.

CLAPBOARD - A long thin board, thicker on one edge, overlapped and nailed on for exterior siding.

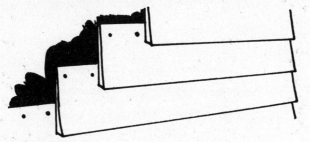

COLLAR BEAM - A horizontal beam fastened above the lower ends of rafters to add rigidity.

CORBEL - A horizontal projection from a wall, forming a ledge or supporting a structure above it.

CORNER BEAD - A strip of wood or metal for protecting the external corners of plastered walls.

CORNICE - Horizontal projection at the top of a wall or under the overhanging part of the roof.

CRAWL SPACE - A shallow, unfinished space beneath the first floor of a house which has no basement, used for visual inspection and access to pipes and ducts. Also a shallow space in the attic, immediately under the roof.

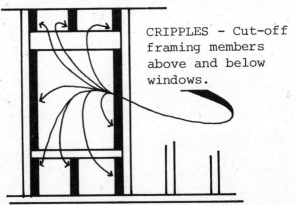

CRIPPLES - Cut-off framing members above and below windows.

DORMER - The projecting frame of a recess in a sloping roof.

DOUBLE HUNG WINDOWS - Windows with an upper and lower sash, each supported by cords and weights.

DRY WALL - A wall surface of plasterboard or material other than plaster.

EAVES - The extension of a roof beyond house walls.

FASCIA - The vertical portion of a soffit or dropped ceiling - the board at the lower edge of a roof line which covers the end of the rafters and to which the gutter is secured.

FILL-TYPE INSULATION - Loose insulating material which is applied by hand or blown into wall spaces mechanically.

FLOOR JOISTS - Framing pieces which rest on outer foundation walls and interior beams or girders.

FRAMING - The rough lumber of a house - joists, studs, rafters and beams.

FURRING - Thin wood or metal applied to a wall to level the surface for lathing, boarding or plastering, to create an insulating air space, and to dampproof the wall.

GABLE - The triangular part of a wall under the inverted "v" of the roof line.

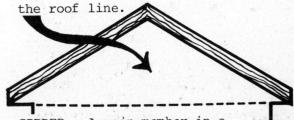

GIRDER - A main member in a framed floor supporting the joists which carry the flooring boards. It carries the weight of a floor or partition.

GRADE LINE - The point at which
the ground rests against the
foundation wall.

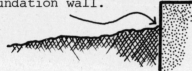

GREEN LUMBER - Lumber which has
been inadequately dried and which
tends to warp or "bleed" resin.

GROUNDS - Pieces of wood embedded in plaster of walls to which
skirtings are attached. Also
wood pieces used to stop the
plaster work around doors and windows.

GUSSET - A brace or bracket used to
strengthen a structure.

HARDWOOD - The close-grained
wood from broad-leaved trees
such as oak or maple.

HEADERS - Double wood pieces
supporting joists in a floor or
double wood members placed on
edge over windows and doors to
transfer the roof and floor
weight to the studs.

HEEL - The end of a rafter
that rests
on the wall plate.

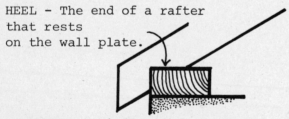

JALOUSIES - Windows with movable
horizontal glass slats angled to
admit ventilation and keep out
rain. This term is also used for
outside shutters of wood constructed in this way.

JAMB - An upright surface that
lines an opening for a door or
window.

JOIST - A small rectangular sec-
tional member arranged parallel
from wall to wall in a building,
or resting on beams or girders.
They support a floor or the laths
or furring strips of a ceiling.

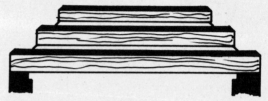

KILN-DRIED - Artificial drying
of lumber, superior to most lumber that is air dried.

LALLY COLUMN - A steel tube sometimes filled with concrete, used
to support girders
or other floor
beams.

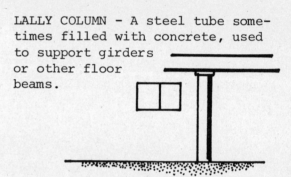

LATH - One of a number of thin
narrow strips of wood nailed to
rafters, ceiling joists, wall studs,
etc. to make a groundwork or key
for slates, tiles or plastering.

LEDGER - A piece of wood which is
attached to a beam to support
joists.

LOUVER - An opening with horizontal slats to permit passage of
air, but excluding rain, sunlight
and view.

MOISTURE BARRIER - Treated paper
or metal that retards or bars
water vapor, used to keep moisture
from passing into walls or floors.

10

MOLDING - A strip of decorative material having a plane or curved narrow surface prepared for ornamental application. These strips are often used to hide gaps at wall junctures.

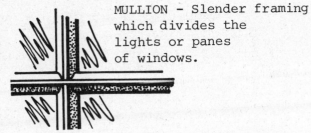

MULLION - Slender framing which divides the lights or panes of windows.

NEWEL - The upright post or the upright formed by the inner or smaller ends of steps about which

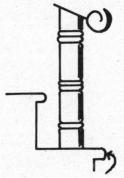

steps of a circular staircase wind. In a straight flight staircase, the principal post at the foot or the secondary post at a landing.

NOSING - The rounded edge of a stair tread.

PARGING - A rough coat of mortar applied over a masonry wall as protection or finish; may also serve as a base for an asphaltic waterproofing compound below grade.

PLASTERBOARD (SEE DRY WALL) - Gypsum board, used instead of plaster.

PREFABRICATION - Construction of components such as walls, trusses or doors before installing in place.

RABBET - A groove cut in a board to receive another board.

RAFTER - One of a series of structural roof members spanning from an exterior wall to a center ridge beam or ridge board.

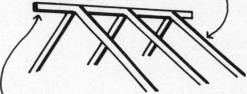

RIDGE POLE - A thick longitudinal plank to which the ridge rafters of a roof are attached.

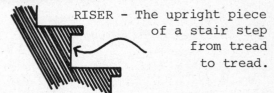

RISER - The upright piece of a stair step from tread to tread.

SANDWICH PANEL - A panel with plastic, paper or other material enclosed between two layers of a different material.

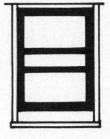

SASH - The movable part of a window--the frame in which panes of glass are set in a window or door.

SHAKES - Handcut wood shingles.

SHEATHING (See Wall Sheathing) - The first covering of boards or material on the outside wall or roof prior to installing the finished siding or roof covering.

SHIM - A thin piece of material (usually wood) used for adjustment purposes when positioning windows and doors.

SHINGLES - Pieces of wood, asbestos or other material used as an overlapping outer covering on walls or roofs.

SHIPLAP - Boards with rabbeted edges overlapping.

SIDING - Boards of special design nailed horizontally to vertical studs with or without intervening sheathing to form the exposed surface of outside walls of frame buildings.

SILL PLATE - The lowest member of the house framing resting on top of the foundation wall. Also called the mud sill.

SKIRTINGS - Narrow boards around the margin of a floor; baseboards.

SLAB - Concrete floor placed directly on earth or a gravel base and usually about four inches thick.

SLEEPER - Strip of wood laid over concrete floor to which the finished wood floor is nailed or glued.

SOFFIT - The visible underside of structural members such as staircases, cornices, beams, a roof overhang or eave.

SOFTWOOD - Easily worked wood or wood from a cone-bearing tree.

STRINGER - A long, horizontal member which connects upright in a frame or supports a floor or the like. One of the enclosed sides of a stair supporting the treads and risers.

STUDS - In wall framing, the vertical members (usually 2 x 4 or 2 x 6) to which horizontal pieces are nailed. Studs are spaced either 16 or 24 inches apart.

SUBFLOOR - Usually, plywood sheets that are nailed directly to the floor joists and that receive the finish flooring.

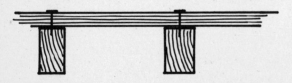

TIE - A wood member which binds a pair of principal rafters at the bottom.

TOENAIL - Nailing at a 45 degree angle through the side of one member into the side of another.

TONGUE-AND-GROOVE - Carpentry joint in which the jutting edge of one board fits into the matching groove end of a similar board.

TREAD - The horizontal part of a stair step.

TRUSS - A combination of structural members usually arranged in triangular units to form a rigid framework for spanning between load-bearing walls.

VAPOR BARRIER - Material such as paper, metal or paint which is used to prevent vapor from passing from rooms into the outside walls.

VENETIAN WINDOW - A window with one large fixed central pane and smaller panes at each side.

WAINSCOTING - The lower 3 or 4 feet of an interior wall when lined with paneling, tile or other material different from the rest of the wall.

WALL SHEATHING - Sheets of gypsum board or other material nailed to studs as a finishing base.

WEATHER STRIPPING - Metal, wood or other material installed around door and window openings to prevent air filtration.

WEEP HOLE - A small hole to permit water to drain off.

Know your materials

STANDARD LUMBER SIZING

Common expressions for lumber sizes do not represent actual measurements. For example, a 2 x 4 currently measures 1 1/2" x 3 1/2". These tables are guides in planning, ordering lumber and when precise cutting and fitting are necessary.

NOMINAL SIZE INCHES	CURRENT SURFACE SIZE INCHES
2 x 2	1 1/2 x 1 1/2
2 x 4	1 1/2 x 3 1/2
2 x 6	1 1/2 x 5 1/2
2 x 8	1 1/2 x 7 1/4
2 x 10	1 1/2 x 9 1/4
2 x 12	1 1/2 x 11 1/4

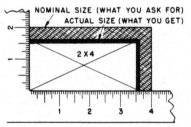

PLANKING AND DECKING

1 x 2	3/4 x 1 1/2
1 x 3	3/4 x 2 1/2
1 x 4	3/4 x 3 1/2
1 x 6	3/4 x 5 1/2

In older houses add 1/8" to each dimension in the table. If very old, 30 or more years, it could measure a fractional 3/4" each way

rather than the present 1/2" or the earlier 5/8".

INSULATION

Available in various types, sizes, materials. Used with walls, joists and attic rafters. Widths match standard construction measurements ... normally 15" to fit between 16 o.c. studs or joists. Available in rolls or pre-cut 8 ft. lengths.

Thickness determines the "R" factor ... "R" being the resistance to thermal flow. Simply stated: heat is energy and it always moves from warm to cold. The greater the difference between inside and outside temperatures, the faster heat will flow out in winter and flow in during summer. Insulation should be selected for the "R" factor that best resists this flow of heat.

Insulation batts and rolls with an attached vapor barrier and stapling flange are stapled between studs on exterior walls ... even when those exterior walls are on the inside of a concrete foundation such as in a basement. The same material is available without a moisture barrier. A 4-mil polyethylene film is used to resist moisture transference.

A 3 1/2" thick fiberglass insulation offers an "R" factor of 11. Six inch fiberglass produces an

Lumber yards often quote prices in board feet. A board foot represents a piece of lumber measuring 12" x 12" x 1" or one square foot one inch thick. To determine the cost, say of an 8-foot length of 2 x 4 quoted at .22 per board foot, locate the nominal size, 2 inches thick and 4 inches wide, on the chart. A 12" length of 2 x 4 is .67 of a board foot. Multiply this by 8 feet (5.36) and then the price of .22 cents. The cost per length is $1.18.

Width	Thickness INCHES											
	1	2	3	4	5	6	7	8	9	10	11	12
2	.17	.33										
3	.25	.5	.75									
4	.34	.67	.1	1.33								
5	.42	.83	1.25	1.67	2.08							
6	.5	1.	1.5	2.	2.5	3.						
7	.59	1.17	1.75	2.33	2.92	3.5	4.08					
8	.67	1.33	2.	2.67	3.33	4.	4.67	5.33				
9	.75	1.5	2.25	3.	3.75	4.5	5.25	6.	6.75			
10	.84	1.67	2.5	3.33	4.17	5.	5.83	6.67	7.5	8.33		
11	.92	1.83	2.75	3.67	4.58	5.5	6.42	7.33	8.25	9.17	10.08	
12	1.	2.	3.	4.	5.	6.	7.	8.	9.	10.	11.	12.

"R" factor of 19 ... and this has normally been the insulation used between attic floor joists. However, the rising costs of energy is forcing some new thinking. In cold climates, "R" factors of 33 to 38 are now recommended and this requires 10 to 12 inches of insulation. "R-26" is now considered minimum for most areas of the country. Joist edges should be covered as they only offer an "R" 3 factor.

SHEET MATERIALS ... PLYWOOD, WOOD AND FIBER PANEL, DRY WALL

The common dimension of sheathing material - drywall, plywood, paneling and hardboard - is 4'x8' and is available in various thicknesses. Hardboard and pegboard come in 1/8" and 1/4"; drywall from 3/8" to a maximum 5/8"; paneling usually is 3/16" while plywood can range from 1/4" to 3/4". It is most important to know the thickness of the original sheathing when making repairs or replacing one or more sheets.

Plywood is available in several grades, various thicknesses and for different kinds of installations. Exterior types ... rated A-A where both facings have a waterproofed glue between plies; must have a good finish. A-B is similar but only one side is intended to show; the other may have patches (boats). A third grade is A-C, good finish one side, rough finish on the reverse side. Two other grades of exterior plywood may have use in certain jobs: (1) C-C plugged ... as a base for floor tile, linoleum or carpeting where an unusual moisture condition exists: (2) C-C, unsanded with waterproof bonding is used as a rough-finished sheathing.

Interior types of plywood use the same grade symbols: A-A and A-B. A third interior classification is commonly referred to as underlayment board and is used as the base for floor tile, linoleum and carpeting where moisture problems are nil.

Paneling in either wood or the more commonly used composition (particle) board, is available in a variety of color tones and finishes. Facings are wood veneer or good duplicates of popular wood grains. Many products are also available with decorative vinyl covering on one side. Moisture conditions and stress will determine the thickness required.

Drywall, also referred to as "gypsum board," is basically plaster covered with a heavy paper on both sides. It is easy to cut, nail, trim. Filling and taping are part and parcel of any drywall installation, so joints at ceiling corners and abutting sheets are less critical than with paneling or fiber board of the same thickness. The lighter shaded side is the facing side.

STANDARD NAIL SIZES

Common nails used in construction:

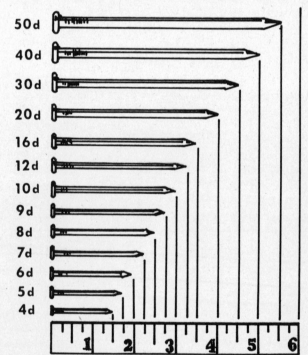

Joist to sill or girder, toe nail 3-8d
Sole plate to blocking or joist, face nail 16" o.c. . . . 16d
Top plate to stud, end nail 2-16d
Stud to sole plate, toe nail 4-8d

14

Continuous header, two pieces
   16" o.c.along each edge   16d
Ceiling joists to plate,
   toe nail 3-8d
Continuous header to stud,
   toe nail 4-8d
Ceiling joists, laps over
   partitions, face nail. . 3-16d
Ceiling joists to parallel
   rafters, face nail . . . 3-16d
Rafter to plate, toe nail . 3-8d

When construction permits lighter
nails, use box nails--about the
same length, but their smaller diameter means more nails to the
pound.

FINISHING NAILS

Finishing nails are used for trim
work and sheathing where the nail
heads are to be recessed for appearance. However, paneling, wall
board and other sheathing can be
fastened directly to most reasonably level wall surface, to studwall framing or furring strips with
paneling adhesives. This offers
advantages over nailing since
counter-sinking the nails and filling the holes with filler is not
necessary.

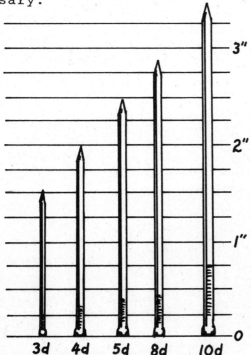

Finishing nails come in fewer
sizes than commons. The small
head is characteristic of all.

Flathead wood screws shown in this
chart are actual size. Length of
flatheads is from the point to
the flat. For roundheads, it is
from point to shoulder. Stores
will have complete range in steel
--most sizes in brass. Marine
stores frequently have a full
range in brass and bronze.

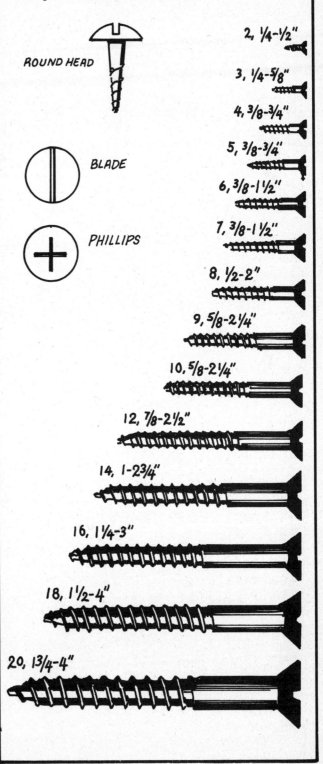

CARPENTRY

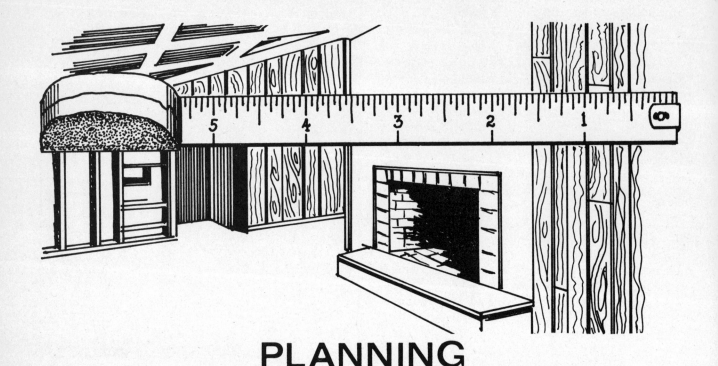

PLANNING

Time will be saved and extra work avoided by analyzing carefully areas that can be improved and then picturing the finished results desired. Two objectives must be considered:

1. Where can added living space be gained.

2. For what primary purposes will the new area be used.

Aside from actually building a new addition on to the house, the attic, garage and basement are usually the best places to consider because of availability of unused space, adequate headroom and ready access. Attics in homes built during the past twenty years often have built-in stairways. Ceiling height is normally adequate for a bedroom and there is some basic framing to work with. Many basements are suitable for recreation or family rooms ... even extra bedrooms ... and a garage can be converted to serve almost any family need.

PRE-PLANNING

Pre-planning is the key to ultimate success in converting an available area into an attractive, functional room. Here are some suggested steps to follow:

1. Study available space, keeping in mind that certain existing structural factors such as waste stacks, drains, windows, supporting beams, columns, bearing walls and utility service entrances can only be moved at great expense because the job usually requires professional skill. Footings and exterior framing for room additions usually fall into the "professional" category for most homeowners, too ... even the handiest!

2. Make a list of all the conveniences to be incorporated into space. In the case of a basement recreation room, consider an enclosed laundry area or workshop, perhaps a half bath. Now is the time to decide.

16

3. A recreation room offers greater opportunity for expressing individual ideas and fun approaches to decorating than other rooms in the house. Some general ideas are outlined in this section, but individual preferences, imagination and experience can easily expand the list. Creating interesting combinations to reflect personal tastes and decor can be fun and personally rewarding. Often, a browsing visit to home improvement or interior decorating departments will stimulate fresh ideas for achieving the over-all effect desired.

4. Consider furniture and decorative items to be included in a family room area. Don't forget storage closets and shelving for books, stereo equipment, planters and other items.

5. Rough measure the area starting with the over-all length and width. Outline the shape on a sheet of graph paper. Let each 1/4" square represent one square foot. Next, indicate the location of columns, existing usable walls, partition walls, plumbing waste stacks, drain lines, electric and gas and water entrances, plus any other obstructions. The sketches of a typical basement and garage show what to include. Attic areas should be treated in the same manner, though fewer obstructions have to be dealt with.

TYPICAL AREA SKETCHES

The exterior walls of a house are fixed so the square footage available is restricted to those dimensions unless a complete room addition is contemplated. Therefore, allotment of space should be approached with care to assure all important facilities are accommodated.

If the garage is to be converted to living area, it is often desirable to raise the floor to the same level or a shallow step down from the adjoining room. To do this, floor joists are set on the concrete floor. Sub-flooring and finish flooring are then added. This will reduce ceiling to floor height, so think it all the way through when planning.

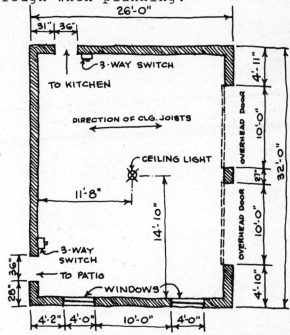

NOTE: SINCE THIS TYPE OF DRAWING IS USED ONLY FOR PLANNING, A ROUGH FREEHAND SKETCH IS SUFFICIENT.

TYPICAL GARAGE SURVEY SKETCH

If an attic is to be converted into additional living area, the over-all dimensions will be limited to the existing headroom unless a dormer is planned.

There are two helpful methods for visualizing actual usable space of different floor plans:

1. Using a chalk line, divide the floor into specific areas of use. Any planned partitioning walls should be indicated with double chalk lines spaced about 5" apart to allow for wall thickness. The area needed for a wet bar must include work space behind the bar plus room for any appliances to be installed now or later. Use blackboard chalk to outline the location of tables, chairs, beds or other furniture which will occupy floor space on a permanent basis. The chalk is easily erased when revising initial plans.

2. The second method is to make scale templates of all the furniture and major decorative items planned for the room. These cutouts can then be moved about on the graph paper layout until the best arrangement has been selected.

Where headroom may be restricted in certain basement and attic areas, make a cross-section drawing of available elevations. Most basement floors have some slope, usually toward the floor drain, so floor to joist heights can vary an inch or more. This cross-section elevation will also help locate on the plan any ceiling obstruction which cannot be moved or modified.

Now go back over the list of conveniences. Can everything be accommodated? The outside dimensions of a large pool table are 6' x 10' with an additional 4 1/2" of clearance needed at the sides and ends. Table tennis tables are usually 4'x9' but 5 or more feet at each end are needed and

and a minimum 2 feet should be allowed for each side. To determine space requirements for furniture items, measure similar size pieces in the home. Wet bars, depending on design, take 5 to 8 feet in depth plus the length desired.

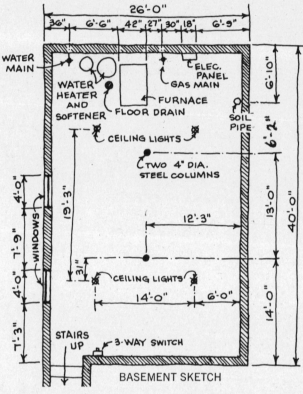

BASEMENT SKETCH

TRACE FOR SCALED TEMPLATES

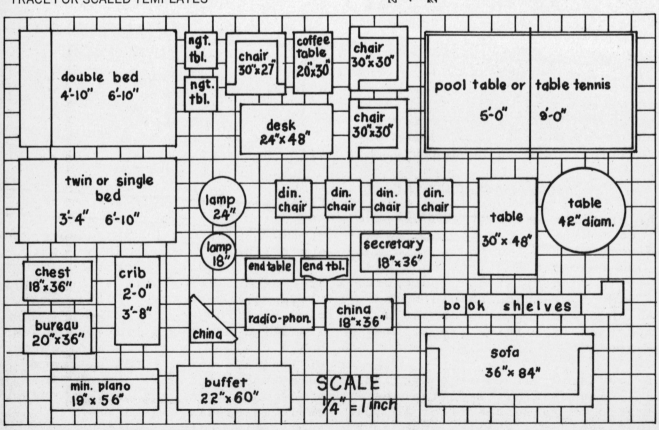

FINAL MEASURING
AND DIAGRAMMING

With ideas formulated and checked against available space, the best plan should be committed to a final drawing that will serve as your guide for the entire construction job.

Carefully re-measure the area. Take basic measurements to the accuracy of 1/4 inch. It will save time, material and frustration to double check all measurements and jot them down immediately. Make a habit of marking these at the point of measurement as well as on the layout. Joists, rough walls and floors will eventually be covered over so marking at the spot serves as a cross-check during construction.

Include wall offsets, outside doors, windows, support columns or walls, beams, waste stacks and pipes, drains, obstructions such as water, gas and electrical service entrances ... anything of a fixed nature. Columns, beams, stacks and pipes should be measured to the center line each way.

In preparing the final layout to an accurate scale, let each 1/4" line on the graph paper represent one foot. If preferred, draw lines to match the grid lines but MAKE CERTAIN THE ACTUAL (TRUE) MEASUREMENTS ARE CLEARLY WRITTEN ON THE LAYOUT.

In the drawing, two windows and a front entrance are built into the garage door opening. The floor can be left at the same level with carpet or tile laid directly on the concrete; or the floor can be raised to the level of the adjoining kitchen floor by use of floor joists and plywood subflooring. Note that the bar sink is connected to the kitchen sink plumbing.

Pre-planning can eliminate many a project problem. In the drawing, the half bath, laundry and bar sink are all located near the existing plumbing stack to simplify their installation. One of the basement I-beam support columns is concealed in the furnace room wall

FINISHED GARAGE LAYOUT

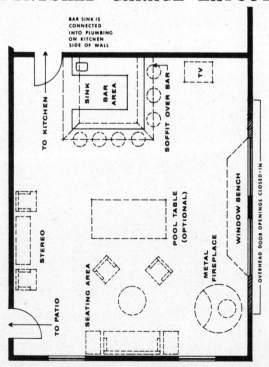

FINISHED BASEMENT LAYOUT

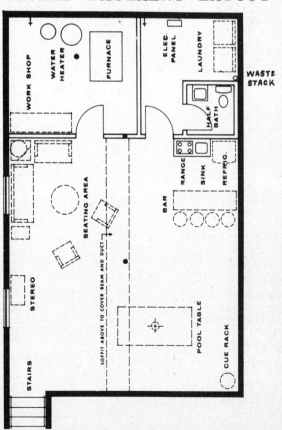

LOCATING PLUMBING

An important consideration during the first planning stages of a recreation room is locating new plumbing requirements close to existing drain facilities. For the do-it-yourself homeowner, this offers more advantages than locating close to a water supply:

1. Drain lines MUST maintain a minimum downward pitch of 1/8" and maximum of 1/4" per lineal foot from the fixture trap to the connecting point with an existing drain. Directional turns should be held to a minimum to assure effective gravity flow.

Water lines, on the other hand, offer considerable flexibility since flow is produced by pressure. Direction can be changed as often as necessary and they can be carried up through the joists and back down to fixtures without loss of effective pressure.

2. The diameter of copper plastic or galvanized drain lines for sinks is usually 1 1/2"; water lines are 3/4", 1/2" and even smaller. The larger pipe size is more expensive per foot so the shorter the run the lower the cost. Furthermore, the job of concealing a drain run within or behind a stud wall increases measurably when branch drains are lengthy.

Bars for home use are available in a wide range of styles, designs and price levels ... both finished and unfinished. Some are free-standing units mounted on casters so they can be moved aside when not being used. A popular arrangement is patterned after the commercial bars ... a front serving bar with stools and a rear deck with sink and cabinet, shelf space for glassware and bar supplies. It provides a convenient way to conceal the fixture trap and drain line while giving easy access to both the trap and water shut-off valves.

HIGH NECK FAUCET FOR BAR

Plans and instructions for building a relatively simple but fully functional bar are explained later.

PLANNING AROUND EXISTING FACILITIES AND OBSTRUCTIONS

Certain residential facilities and obstructions can be moved to accommodate plans; others cannot be moved without considerable trouble or expense. These next paragraphs show how attractive and useful living space can be achieved at the lowest possible cost. The key is knowing which common facilities can be moved or modified and those that usually should remain as they are:

CAN BE RELOCATED

Non-bearing walls

Branch heating ducts

Water lines

Electrical lines

Washers, dryers, sinks

DIFFICULT TO RELOCATE

Furnace

Main heating ducts, chimneys ... most of these are closely identified with basement areas; however, attics and garages can be affected by one or more.

Waste stacks, floor drains, sump pumps

Water heater, water softener

Electrical, water, gas entrances

Bearing walls, columns, beams, joists

Stairways, windows, outside doors

To reduce material costs and save valuable space, take advantage of existing facilities. For example, can a half bath addition or wet bar sink be conveniently located near the waste stack? Can a partitioning wall be positioned to hide a column or beam, thus saving material and time to box it in? A seat built around a support column can be functional as well as decorative. Consider alternatives NOW!

BASEMENT CROSS-SECTION

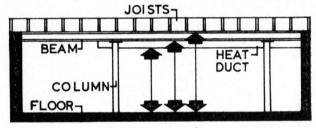

If beams, columns and stacks have to be boxed in, perhaps some electrical wiring, water lines or gas piping hanging below the ceiling joists can be re-routed to gain extra headroom and a level ceiling. Review the cross-section sketch in "Planning."

MAINTAINING REQUIRED ACCESSES

For obvious reasons of safety, utility and emergency protection, certain permanent installations in and around the home must be easily identified and quickly accessible by all members of the family or such emergency personnel as the police, firemen or gas and electric company servicemen. These installations are:

Gas main and branch valves

Electrical entrance panel

Oil-line shut-off valves if oil heated

Ductwork dampers

Water main and branch valves

Sump pumps

Tag and identify each one before starting construction and also identify them accurately on the drawing! Remember to provide for access when finishing walls and installing ceilings.

Duct work may have dampers for directing heat into the proposed room area. If the heat radiated from the exposed heating ducts is adequate, the ducts can be framed out with wood and covered with decorative metal grillwork on the sides and bottom to maintain heat radiation. In some instances, it may be best to plan for supplemental heat ... gas or electric ... but first investigate the possibility of connecting the existing system. Check to see if it has enough reserve capacity for the added load.

Does it heat/cool each room adequately, even in extremes of temperature? An added room area can increase the demand load by 25% or more. If in doubt, check this out with a recognized heating contractor. A larger blower unit or perhaps a separate source for the new area may be required.

Also consider the difficulty in connecting into the present system. A forced air system involves cutting openings and pathways for the new hot air and cold air return ducts. Hydronic and steam systems involve piping and radiators.

Just about any problem can be solved, but know how much the total investment will be ... before signing papers.

If connecting onto the existing heating/cooling system should prove impractical, consider these alternatives:

Gas heating - in-the-wall heater units or a gas fireplace with blower.

Electric - small baseboard units or electric fireplace with blower.

No matter what you select, be sure to have your supplier "size" the unit according to your needs. It is frustrating to build or revamp a room only to find it cannot be used at times because of inadequate heating/cooling.

WALLS

The choice of wall treatment is almost unlimited and creativity can be expressed to its fullest. Here are just a few possibilities and some variations which can be used in toto or as combinations:

CONCRETE

Painted or muraled

Painted and decorated with mod or travel posters, framed or not

Painted white or a soft pastel with rough cedar or similar wood boards stained a dark brown and mounted so as to depict a chalet or old world pub decor. Boards are anchored to the concrete. A groove channeled in the back can carry wire to lights or wall outlets.

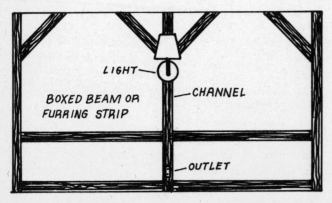

LIGHT

BOXED BEAM OR FURRING STRIP

CHANNEL

OUTLET

Painted, with colored ropes running across the wall face in an open or tight design with direction changes secured by large eye hooks.

Resurfaced with a cement-paint mixture. Decor highlights, such as bright stones, can be embedded in the new surface before it sets up.

PANELS — BOARDS

Standard 4 x 8 ft. sheets in veneer or photographed grained finishes.

An exterior grade plywood can be used when a woody look is desired at a cost less than wood paneling boards. It is installed like regular paneling ... can be stained or shellacked and then varnished. Peg board has many uses ... particularly as a partitioning wall enclosing a furnace area. The holes let sufficient air get to pass through to the room areas adjacent. It can be painted or left natural. It, too, is installed like paneling.

Tongue and groove random-length boards in any number of grains and finishes ... rough sawn or smooth; weathered barn siding or crating lumber.

CLOTH

Burlap, canvas, tenting or carpeting.

Carpet manufacturers offer a carpeting especially for wall covering. It has lightweight backing to reduce weight, yet gives a very plush appearance. It can be tacked or glued to a drywall underlayment. One advantage is it reduces noise levels considerably and cleaning is simple ... merely vacuum.

An attractive feature wall can be created by painting drywall panels or concrete a dark blue, green or

black and then mounting vertical
2 x 2's or 1 x 2's about one inch
apart. The wood strips are sealed
with shellac, smoothed with steel
wool or fine sandpaper. Finish
with a clear varnish for a natural
wood or paint a contrasting tone
to the background color. It is
particularly good for creating a
sense of depth to a narrow room or
walled area.

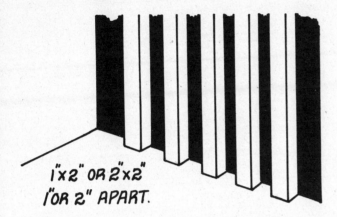

1"x2" OR 2"x2"
1"OR 2" APART.

Using this list as a starting point
browse through home improvement and
interior decorating departments for
more ideas on colors and combinations of materials available
to achieve the right look. Test
several combinations until the desired effect is obtained. Whether
early American, traditional, modern or something very individual,
the mood and decor will be set by
the choice of wall finish and effective use of lighting.

NOTE: AS A GENERAL RULE, IT IS
BEST TO INSTALL A FURRED AND TILED
CEILING BEFORE WALLS ARE INSTALLED.
IT IS EASIER TO CUT TOP EDGES ON
WALL PANELING THAN INDIVIDUAL 12
X 12 INCH TILES AROUND AN ENTIRE
WALL.

BECAUSE WALL ANGLE IS MOUNTED ON
THE FINISHED WALL, WITH A SUSPEND-
ED CEILING THE WALLS ARE COMPLETED
FIRST.

CEILINGS

Ceiling and good lighting set the
mood of a room. Variations in
treatment are not as broad as in

wall treatment, but there are
enough choices to justify careful
planning before starting.

WHAT KIND OF CEILING?

SHEATHING

Drywall - taped and painted

Beaver board - natural or painted

Peg board - natural or painted

Plywood - stained or painted

TILING

12" x 12" or 12" x 24" acoustical
tiles glued or stapled to furring
strips or glued to drywall

2' x 2' or 2' x 4' suspended
panels in a grid frame

OTHERS

Lattice strips - nailed to joists;
joist recess is painted

Burlap, canvas, tenting or net-
ting - fireproofed

Colored rope - run across joists
in close sequence

Cork sheets - usually glued to
drywall

Plaster - rough or smooth finish

Before any work is started on walls
or ceilings, it is necessary to
know:

1. Floor to joist clearance. Normal ceiling headroom in a basement
recreation room, ground level family room or attic bedroom is
usually about 7 feet; it can always be more or a bit less. Where
clearance is at or near this minimum, the choice of ceiling material is limited to (1) drywall
sheathing nailed directly to the
joists, then taped and painted or
left unfinished as a base for
glueing ceiling tile; (2) nailed

across the joists to provide solid base for stapling tile squares or panels in place.

2. The distance the ceiling can be dropped below joist level to conceal all or most of the pipes and other obstructions hanging below joists.

Considerable extra work is eliminated when the ceiling can be dropped to a level that conceals pipes and other obstructions which protrude below joist level. To gain extra drop, furring strips can first be nailed <u>along</u> the bottom of the joist with a second strip then nailed across as previously described. This will gain 3/4" additional drop for concealing many "underhangs."

Perpendicular nailing strips are usually not necessary since most joists are spaced 16" on center and the 4' x 8' sheets can be nailed directly to the joists. If joists are on 24" centers, then furring strips must first be spaced across the joists on 16" centers to provide a nailing surface for the sheathing material. Anything that cannot be concealed above the ceiling level can be framed out and covered with fitted pieces of the ceiling material ... or painted to blend in.

When 7'2" or more headroom is available, a suspended grid frame system can be installed. Many homeowners find this the easiest installation since far less overhead nailing is required. When the runners, cross-tees and angles have been installed, the ceiling panels are merely placed on the frames. Both the grid and furring methods will be discussed later.

To prevent sagging over the years, the drywall for ceilings should be 5/8" thick. Cracks between abutting edges and surface dents must be filled and taped when the drywall surface will be merely painted and not covered with a layer of tile or other material.

Noise absorbing, heat retaining insulation is generally desirable between joist and stud members. The heat and cooling retention qualities of 3" thick x 15" wide batts in all outside walls, roof rafters and ceiling joists is a "must" for attic and garage areas and highly recommended for basements. Where an added noise barrier is desirable, use drywall as a base for ceiling tile.

LIGHTING TREATMENT

Electrical wiring should be planned for adequate lighting and wall outlets. If a basement ceiling is to be finished but the walls left in natural concrete, wiring can be carried in the joists above and brought down inside decorative boxed columns for wall outlets or switches. If a 2 x 4 stud wall is to be paneled or drywalled, wiring can be routed through the studs to various junction boxes.

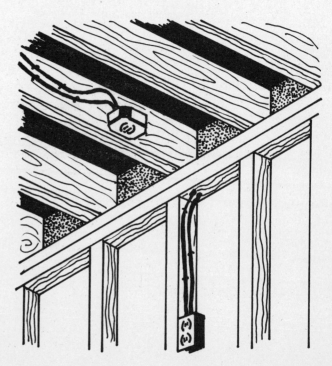

Lighting should be considered from both a functional and decorative standpoint ... the possibilities are unlimited today. If headroom is low, use fixtures that mount flush with the ceiling between joists. There is also a wide variety of ceiling-mounted and hanging fixtures available for areas with the necessary headroom. Spotlights can be used effectively to highlight objects or focus attention on certain areas.

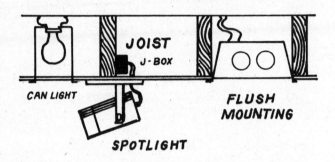

Heat lamps can be used in special types of fixtures and provide both light and additional heat in a limited area. Replace heat bulb with standard light bulb during summer. Wall-mounted lights add decor and can also brighten a reading area. Various fixtures can be controlled by a dimmer switch and allows lighting, as the occasion suggests. Lighting requirements and preference can govern choice of both wall and ceiling treatments so both must be considered during early planning.

Many new lighting products are being developed and introduced regularly, so spend some time looking at styles and prices in electrical fixture departments. It can pay!

FLOOR COVERING

Selection of floor covering best suited for an area is a matter of personal choice but it will help to know some of the characteristics of materials available today.

Floor covering divides into two main categories: Hard surface and soft surface.

HARD SURFACE

Deck Paint - oil or water base

Wood - Tongue and groove boards or plywood sheets nailed to 2 x 4 or 2 x 6 flooring frames ... good for basements with dry floor and high ceiling.

Wood platform (open construction) as used behind bars and other potentially wet floor areas.

Parquet 12 x 12 wood tiles. Oak hardwood flooring over sub-floor. Both are very expensive.

Linoleum - 3' to 12' widths - some have a cellular rubber backing for resiliency underfoot and to act as an insulation between concrete and linoleum surface.

Tile squares - 12" x 12": vinyl - pure; vinyl asbestos; asphalt.

SOFT SURFACE

Carpeting - 9' and 12' widths: Indoor/outdoor - felt; indoor/outdoor - piled.

Carpet squares (12" x 12", 15" x 15" or 18" x 18"): Pressed felt; piled - tufted or looped

Carpet squares sometimes have a quick release backing that eliminates special mastic; others have a cellular rubber backing that is coated with a special mastic that allows taking up and putting back individual squares.

Before making a choice, three factors should be considered:

1. The primary use of the room - a game and play area for children, an entertainment center, a family room for day-to-day comfort, added or convertible bedroom space. The area may have to serve a combination of purposes.

2. Moisture conditions - both in winter and summer months. Supplemental heat may change humidity levels in winter months but does not affect those conditions in summer.

3. Freedom from maintenance desired.

Some tile and linoleum products require regular maintenance and waxing while others only need a damp mopping to retain their appearance. High traffic areas always need more attention ... especially when some of that traffic is directly from out-of-doors.

CONSIDERATIONS

Both hard and soft surface floor coverings are available in varying grades. Limiting factors are cost, potential moisture problems and room use. Sometimes a combination of materials can serve various functions and create a very interesting effect in conjunction with selective lighting.

DECK PAINT

Several coats of a good deck paint or epoxy applied over a good prime coat. It should then be varnished. Nevertheless, deck paint is difficult to maintain in high traffic areas. Re-painting is required periodically. If employed as a temporary measure and tile will eventually be laid, avoid oil base paints. Certain adhesives used with tile can cause a chemical change in the old paint and it will eventually seep up between the tiling squares.

LINOLEUM

Linoleum is now available in narrow and standard widths for easy handling and installation by the homeowner. Special seam sealers to blend abutting strips to give the appearance of a seamless floor covering. Linoleum backed with cellular rubber should be limited to dry areas. Masonry floors should be sealed first.

TILE SQUARES

12" x 12" tile cemented to clean, sealed floor or cemented to a sound sub-flooring. Thickness of the tile is one measure of durability, and either 3/32" or 1/8" is recommended. A 1/16" is available but the thicker tile offers better resistance to curling, chipping and cracking.

ACTUAL THICKNESS

1/16"	3/32"	1/8"

Pure vinyl is expensive by comparison to other hard surface materials but it offers excellent durability. Damp mopping takes care of most maintenance. It retains luster and color for years because color and design run through the full thickness. However, it tends to shrink with age.

Vinyl asbestos is next in durability but waxing is required to keep it bright and clean looking. It is less expensive than pure vinyl.

Asphalt is a low-luster tile material which no amount of waxing will change measurably. It is difficult to maintain, and scuff marks and stains are hard to remove. It is very practical in utility areas like a laundry room, furnace or workshop. Cutting requires heating the tile first. A Type Z cutback mastic is used to cement asphalt. When it has set, removal is a tedious chore.

Indoor/Outdoor squares or laying widths on sealed masonry floor to firm underlayment. Either self-stick or spot glued.

Regular carpeting or padding over sub-flooring in moisture-free area such as an attic or a garage conversion with a raised floor.

New man-made fibers and adhesives have broadened the uses for carpeting or soft floor surfaces. Carpet squares, a development that certainly benefits the do-it-yourselfer, offer a wide selection of colors and patterns in regular carpet or the indoor/outdoor materials. Tufted, looped or random sheared carpeting offers sound absorbing qualities as well as comfort underfoot and a warmer surface for children. Smooth (pressed felt) carpeting is generally less expensive but is hard to vacuum and may not be stain resistant. Both can be effectively combined with tile for seating and "feature" areas.

Manufacturers specify the mastic for use with their product. Floor covering suppliers will figure the amount of material needed to complete the area based on measurements provided by the customer. As a general rule, an extra 10% should be ordered when tile squares are used to assure even bordering on opposite walls and for replacing damaged tiles later. Detailed installation instructions for the material selected is also available.

USE THIS SCALE GRID TO OUTLINE THE AREA

1/8 Inch Scale   DIAGRAMS   1/8 Inch Scale

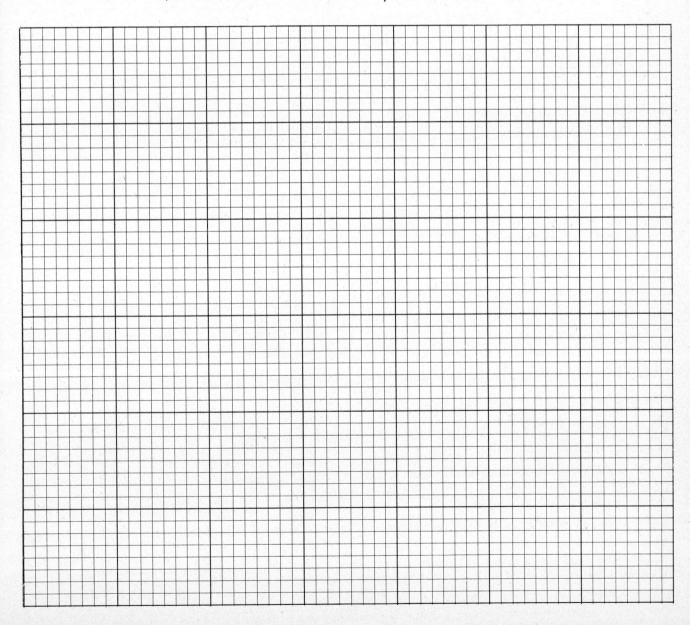

WOOD FRAMING

It is important to control expenses in this area. Know what materials to order and the quantities needed to complete the job. Draw up an order list ... indicate sizes, number of pieces or board feet and cost. Watch for "specials." Buy the best lumber available for framing. It's worth it! Millwork will be true nominal measurements but "yard cut" can vary.

Hand pick lumber to be stained or left natural. Construction Grade is fine for rough framing and work to be covered. Lumber should be stored flat on supporting blocks ... not on the floor or leaning against a wall. Use enough supports to prevent sagging.

1. Floor to ceiling height in most homes today is 8 feet or less, so 2 x 4 studs are usually bought in 7'9" or 8' lengths. If the basement or attic ceiling height is less, there will be more scrap pieces, but don't be in a hurry to toss them away ... many will be usable for horizontal blocking, electrical junction box supports, bracing, and cripples.

Studs for both partitioning and furring are placed 16" on center with double studding at corners and each side of doors and windows. To estimate the number of 8' studs needed, measure the to-tal length of all new walls to be constructed. Convert the total footage into inches, multiplying by 12". Divide this total by 16" to determine basic stud requirements. Add enough extra studs for divider and partition walls, corners, doors and windows. Order plenty because the need will usually be found for several extra lengths when framing a room area.

2. Requirements for top and bottom plates are figured by using the same perimeter measurements plus the length of partition walls and then multiply by 2. This is the approximate linear footage needed for top and bottom plates. These can be ordered in 7'9" or longer lengths ... divide by the total footage of the selected length to determine the approximate number of pieces needed.

```
┌─────────────────────────────────┐
│          QUICK ESTIMATOR        │
│                                 │
│    Plate              Number    │
│    Length             of Studs  │
│                                 │
│     8' 0"                7      │
│     9' 4"                8      │
│    10' 8"                9      │
│    12' 0"               10      │
└─────────────────────────────────┘
```

Plate Length	Number of Studs
8' 0"	7
9' 4"	8
10' 8"	9
12' 0"	10

If a long wall run measures 23 or 24 feet, 12 foot 2 x 4's as plates will reduce waste, but keep in mind the job of getting the lumber into the house and possibly around a tight corner or two. Prefab wall sections longer than 8 to 10 feet are difficult to raise into place alone. With direct wall construction, the plates can be any length. Study all lumber requirements carefully. It can save both money and labor.

3. ORDER ENOUGH. Don't go short on the basics.

PANELING, DRYWALL AND PLYWOOD

1. Most wall and ceiling sheathing comes in 4 x 8 foot sheets. Only thickness varies. To determine the number of 4'x 8' sheets required, use the linear measurements of the walls in feet and divide by 4 feet. Figure each wall section separately, not a total of all walls. If a long wall is 23 or 24 feet, six sheets are needed; a short wall 14 feet long, order four sheets. It is best to order 2 or 3 extra sheets for trimming out over windows and doors, in recessed windows, offset walls, etc. Two door or window openings can reduce the number of sheets needed by one.

2. Store all sheathing flat on four spaced 4' 2 x 4's on edge ... and, to protect from scratches leave on any wrappings until ready to use.

PRE-HUNG DOORS

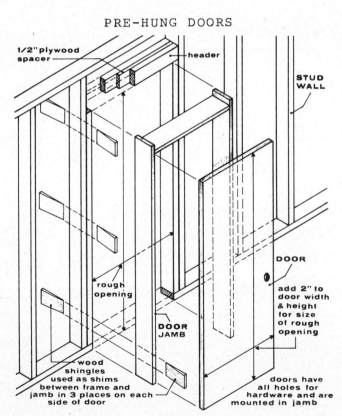

1/2"plywood spacer

header

STUD WALL

DOOR

add 2" to door width & height for size of rough opening

rough opening

DOOR JAMB

wood shingles used as shims between frame and jamb in 3 places on each side of door

doors have all holes for hardware and are mounted in jamb

The standard door is 6'8" high. If the door is too high for the opening, it can be cut off at the bottom without impairing the door action at all. About 3/4" of the jamb can be cut off at the top if additional clearance is needed for proper fit. Usually low height doors can be "special ordered" from most lumber yards at additional cost.

Standard widths include 16, 18, 24, 28, 30, 32, 34 and 36 inches. A primary consideration, particularly in a basement area, is what will have to pass through the opening. A door to a furnace room should be adequate to permit easy passage of appliances.

When ordering, give the measurements of the door opening, the side to be hinged and the direction of swing. Write this data on the floor plan for future reference.

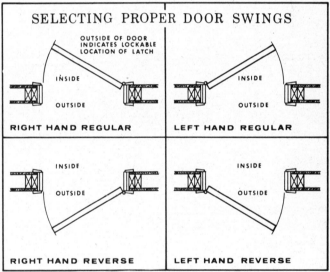

SELECTING PROPER DOOR SWINGS

OUTSIDE OF DOOR INDICATES LOCKABLE LOCATION OF LATCH

INSIDE / OUTSIDE — RIGHT HAND REGULAR

INSIDE / OUTSIDE — LEFT HAND REGULAR

INSIDE / OUTSIDE — RIGHT HAND REVERSE

INSIDE / OUTSIDE — LEFT HAND REVERSE

ESTIMATING NAIL REQUIREMENTS BY SIZE AND USE

1. The key to ordering nails is to order enough. About a pound for each 10 studs. They're not expensive and it is frustrating to run out in the middle of an evening's work. Watch the supply.

2. Coated box nails are less likely to split the wood as they are thinner than common nails. Moistening or soaping shanks also helps prevent splitting. The full head makes a good target and the coating helps the nail hold while reducing the likelihood of rust stains where dampness is prevalent.

3. Use 12d nails for toe nailing studs to a plate. Use masonry nails, lead anchors or power stud gun to fasten base plates to a concrete floor. Space masonry nails every 3 feet to 4 feet along plate.

4. If a stud wall is constructed on the floor and then raised into position, use 16d nails for end nailing because the length is needed to drive through the plate and into the stud end. Two nails should be used at each stud joint.

5. For drywall, beaver board, plywood, etc.: a rule of thumb is 30 to 40 nails per sheet of 4 x 8. Nail size required varies with thickness of the panel:

3/8" wall board...1 1/8" annular nails

1/2" wall board...1 1/4" annular nails

1/4" wall board...1 3/8" annular nails

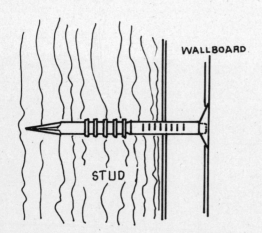

6. Finishing nails are used on paneling and trim work. However, paneling, wall board and other materials can also be fastened directly to a level wall surface or directly to stud wall framing with paneling adhesive ... or, it may be glued to an undersheet of drywall. This method of application offers advantages over nailing because it saves counter-setting the nails and filling the holes with matching filler.

CHECK LIST
MATERIALS & SUPPLIES

(Check Tool List, Too!)

LUMBER	QUANTITY	LENGTH
1 x 3	_____	_____
1 x 4	_____	_____
2 x 2	_____	_____
2 x 4	_____	_____
2 x 6	_____	_____
2 x 8	_____	_____
2 x 10	_____	_____
2 x 12	_____	_____

MOLDING	FEET	STYLE
¼ Round	_____	_____
½ Round	_____	_____
Baseboard	_____	
Base Shoe	_____	
Cove	_____	
Casing	_____	
Corner	_____	

SHEET MATERIAL

Drywall	_____
Paneling	_____
Plywood	_____
Pegboard	_____
Fiberboard	_____

NAILS & FASTENERS	LBS
Common	
16d	_____
12d	_____
8d	_____
Finish	
8d	_____
4d	_____
Drywall	_____
Paneling	_____
Concrete	_____
Tacks/brads	_____
Staples	_____
Anchor Bolts	_____
Adhesive	_____

SUPPLIES

Insulation	_____
Shim Shingles	_____
Polyethylene	_____
Drywall Tape	_____
Drywall Compound	_____
Corner Bead	_____
Buckets/Trays	_____
Sandpaper	_____
Masking tape	_____
Chalk/Pencil	_____

OTHER

Pre-Hung Doors/Windows	_____
Ceiling Tile 12"x12"	_____
Suspended Ceiling	
Elements	_____
Wire	_____
Panels 2'x4'	_____

TESTING

Grabbing a "hot" wire by mistake does not make a better electrician ... just a smarter one. Whenever in doubt about a circuit wire or outlet, TEST IT FIRST WITH A CIRCUIT TESTER.

VENTILATION

When painting or using adhesive, work with an open window. Dust from sawing or sanding can be controlled with a workshop vacuum or a canister-type home vacuum with a large funnel-shaped intake attached to the vacuum hose and suspended above the work area.

FIRST AID

Purchase a good first aid kit and keep it handy. Wear goggles when using a power saw, drilling into concrete or metal, hammering over head. Be deliberate in making decisions. Avoid getting in a hurry because "haste makes waste" of time and material. Haste also causes accidents. Plan out the work that can easily be accomplished in an evening and STOP! It is better to take an extra day or so to finish the job than to spend those days or more recovering from an avoidable accident. Maintain a comfortable construction schedule and don't work when overly tired. By planning the job in stages, a few days of rest can be scheduled between each stage. Ask for help when four hands are needed. Don't try to improvise a shortcut method for two hands.

CHOOSE YOUR NEXT LADDER WITH THE COLOR CODE SYSTEM

Selecting the right ladder for do-it-yourself projects is easy under the coding system manufacturers have adopted.

A RED label indicates a Type III ladder. In wood, this means the ladder is designed for general household purposes; if metal, the ladder is designed for light duty use.

Metal ladders are lightweight and easy to carry, and are less affected by weather. Wood is recommended for use near electricity.

HOW TO USE A LADDER

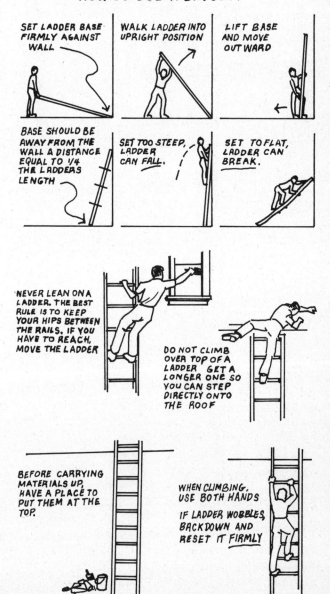

CARPENTRY

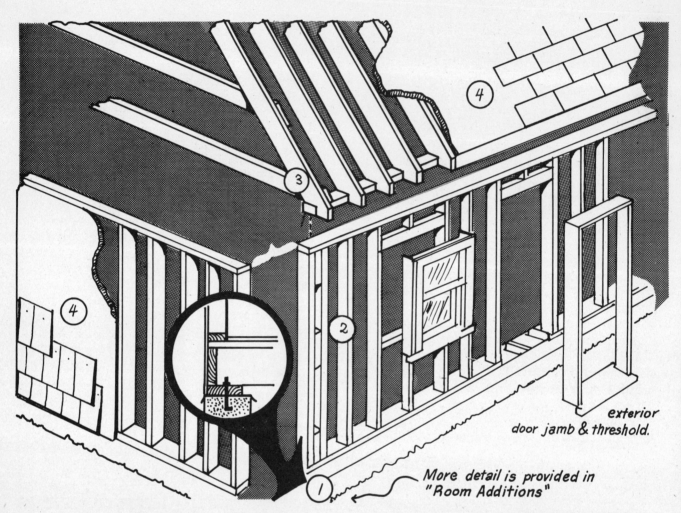

exterior
door jamb & threshold.

More detail is provided in
"Room Additions"

In its simplest form, a house is a series of related elements tied together with nails. To understand this fact, examine the illustration. (1) The foundation supports the outside walls and keeps everything in place; (2) the outside walls accommodate windows and doors; (3) the roof rafters rest on the upper walls; (4) sheathing, such as exterior grade plywood, is used to close in the walls and roof. Ultimately, an outside finish is added in siding, brick veneer or similar finish and the roof is shingled.

Whether present plans call for carpentry-type improvements or not, this chapter and the chapter on finishing provide much

useful know-how. Understanding ... how studs are spaced, where blocking and other cross members are usually located, basic door and window framing ... the homeowner can handle most projects.

For instance, know what might be found behind the existing wall surface and many jobs can be done faster, easier and better ... like locating a stud in order to hang a heavy mirror or picture; securing shelf brackets, bookshelves and cabinets; easing sticking doors and windows; repairing drywall; installing paneling; changing unused basement area into a family recreation room or even a garage into bedrooms; building a workroom; even enclosing a laundry or workshop area; undertake other home improvement projects like a closet. This know-how can also be helpful in evaluating basic value of a house for sale.

If you want to know what some part of a house structure is called, check Know Your House.

COMMON STUD WALL FRAMING ELEMENTS

Construction of a wall is quite simple. It involves four basic steps: (a) careful measuring; (b) transferring those measurements to the wood members to be cut; (c) sawing; (d) nailing the elements together.

The principal wood members which make up a wall are: (1) Top and bottom plates; (2) vertical studs.

A typical stud wall section is illustrated. Note the two plates which hold everything in place and the studs which provide vertical strength and a nailing surface when attaching wall sheathing such as drywall, paneling, etc. If it were a loadbearing wall such as a perimeter wall or interior structural wall, a double top plate (two horizontal plates nailed together) would be employed. Most residential walls are constructed of standard 2 x 4's but special purpose walls utilizing 2 x 6's are sometimes used to accommodate plumbing pipes or oversized duct runs.

When a wall run is interrupted by a door or window, several other framing members come into use: (3) door or window header to absorb the weight load above the opening; (4) cripples (a trade term for a partial stud - less than full length) used to hold the headers in place; (5) blocking ... any horizontal member placed between two or more studs falls under the broad classification of blocking.

Medicine cabinet and shelf blocking is nailed flush with the facing edge of the studs, flat side forward. Blocking for support of a bathroom lavatory is fastened the same way. It can be a 2 x 4 or 2 x 6 nailed between

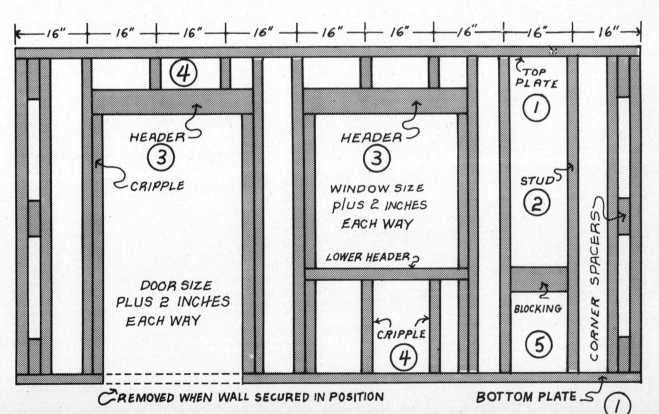

DOOR SIZE PLUS 2 INCHES EACH WAY

WINDOW SIZE plus 2 INCHES EACH WAY

LOWER HEADER

HEADER ③ CRIPPLE ④

HEADER ③

CRIPPLE ④

TOP PLATE ①

STUD ②

BLOCKING ⑤

CORNER SPACERS

REMOVED WHEN WALL SECURED IN POSITION

BOTTOM PLATE ①

the studs where the fixture is
to be mounted. Manufacturers
include instructions for blocking size and height with their
fixtures.

In some areas of the country,
fire stops are required. They
are 2 x 4's nailed between all
concealed studs in a home to
prevent the spread of fire and
smoke inside the wall. They
should fit tight ... whereas
blocking can merely fit the
space.

LAYOUT FOR A BASIC WALL

Stud walls are laid out in a standard stud pattern. Various stud
positions are then modified to in-
corporate the desired changes.

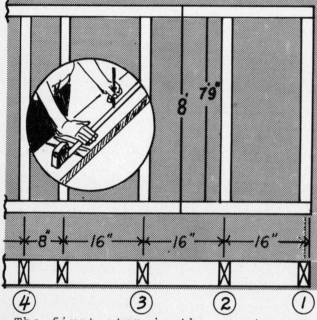

④   ③   ②   ①

The first step in the construction of a wall is the marking of
stud locations on the top and bottom plates. Select straightest
2 x 4's for the plates. If wall
section is less than a full stud
length, cut the plates to the desired length. Lay plates side by
side and mark correct stud locations on both plates at the same
time to minimize measurement errors.

(1) The first stud is placed on
the end of the plate. (2) The
center of the second stud is lo-

cated 16" o.c. (on center) from
the <u>outside</u> <u>edge</u> of the first
stud. Look at the illustration.
(3) The center of the third stud
and each succeeding stud is set
on 16" centers. (4) The last
stud may fall less but never more
than 16" from the center of the
previous stud.

When constructing a wall, <u>remember</u>
that <u>stud</u> <u>lengths</u> are less than
the height of the proposed fi-
nished wall. For example, an 8
ft. interior wall using standard
1 1/2" x 3 1/2" studs and plates
takes studs 7'9" or 93" long because the combined thickness of
the plates is 3 inches. Studs
pre-cut to 7'9" lengths are
available from lumber yards.

MODIFICATION FOR AN OBSTRUCTION

Some rooms and most basements have obstructions, such as ductwork, beams, pipes or wiring, which hang below the ceiling joists. If they cannot be moved, you will have to consider them when building a wall section. Modification of the wall (top plate and affected studs) is done as the section is built.

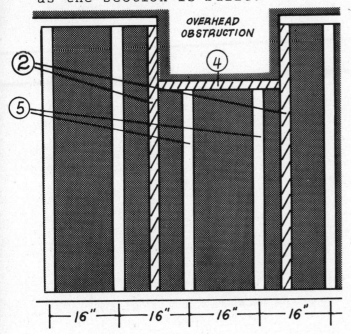

When framing around a ceiling obstruction, an extra vertical stud must be inserted on each side of the obstruction.

Follow these steps:

1. Measure from last fixed wall section or corner (a) the distance to the obstruction and (b) the width of the obstruction. Locate where this will fall on the top and bottom plates, and mark accordingly.

2. Position and nail additional studs on each side of the obstruction as the wall section is prefabbed. Omit 16" o.c. studs that fall within the area below the obstruction opening; however, have the correct 16" o.c. positions marked on both plates for later reference.

3. Measure and mark depth of obstruction opening on the added studs (#2).

4. Measure and cut a cross block and nail in place between the studs used in framing out the sides of the opening.

5. Add necessary 2 x 4 cripples between cross block and bottom plate where any 16" o.c. studs would have normally been positioned (#2).

6. When prefabbing the section, cut out top plate through the obstruction before raising wall into position.

MODIFICATIONS FOR A CORNER

A common modification to any perimeter wall occurs where two walls meet at a corner. An extra stud is added to the end of one of the wall sections to provide a nailing surface for the material to be used for the finished wall.

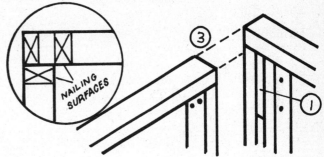

An easy way to determine just where to insert the extra stud is illustrated: (1) Position three short 2 x 4 spacer blocks (at top, center and bottom) between the end stud on the wall section and the extra stud. End nail the stud top and bottom. (2) Use 2 - 12d nails, driving through the extra stud into each spacer. The second wall need not be modified until it reaches a corner position. (3) The two wall sections should be nailed together with 12d nails - two at the top, middle and bottom where they abut. Make sure the single stud wall section is positioned over the section with the extra stud. Note inset in illustration.

MODIFICATIONS FOR A "T" WALL

A wall section that abuts another wall at some mid-point is referred to as a "T" wall. The "T" wall is <u>not modified</u>, but the wall to which it connects requires modification to facilitate tying the two sections together and later providing a nailing surface for the wall sheathing at the corner created by the "T" wall.

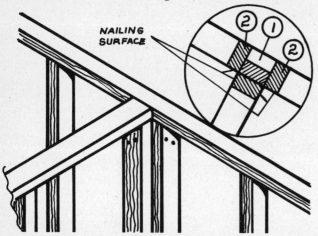

(1) A stud must be set where the "T" wall is to join. This stud is usually placed sideways (rotated 90 degrees) and set at the edge of the plate so that its 3 1/2" side will butt the end stud of the "T" wall. See inset illustration.
(2) A stud is then nailed to each side of the first added stud to create the necessary faces for the sheathing. Nail these studs with 12d nails. As with a corner, the "T" wall is then nailed in place in three locations with 12d nails.

MODIFICATIONS FOR FRAMING A DOOR OR WINDOW OPENING

Except for the addition of the stool section for a window opening, the framing for a door or a window is the same. The basic elements are the stud and cripple on each side of the opening. A window requires a stool nailed across the bottom of the rough-in opening. All 16" o.c. studs that would normally fall within the opening are deleted. Headers and header cripples complete the fram-

ing. H O W recommends using pre-hung doors and windows. A prehung unit is purchased to size as an assembled unit, complete with trim and ready to be set into the opening. The savings in both time and irritation can make the small added cost of the prehung worthwhile.

Standard doors are 6'8" high and whatever width is desired. Widths are usually referred to in feet and inches ... a 2-6 door is 2 feet six inches wide ... a 3-0 is 3 feet wide, etc.

ROUGH FRAMING A DOOR OPENING

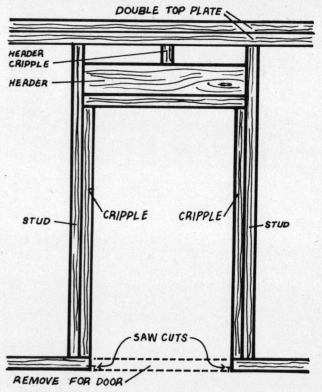

1. Measure the over-all width of the door, including jamb and add 1/4 to 1/2 inch for working room. This should equal the width of the door plus 2" and represents the measurement between the cripples supporting the door header.

Mark the location of the cripples and door studs on both the top and bottom plates. Normally it is advisable to leave the bottom plate of the wall in place until the wall is assembled and secured into position. However, a 1/2" saw cut <u>from the bottom side</u> of the plate will facilitate removal of that plate section later.

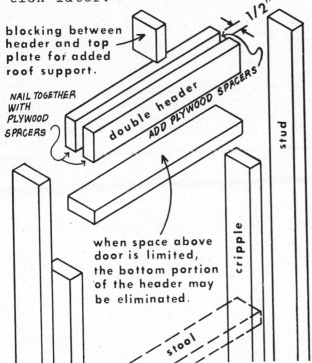

blocking between header and top plate for added roof support.

NAIL TOGETHER WITH PLYWOOD SPACERS

double header

ADD PLYWOOD SPACERS

1/2"

stud

cripple

when space above door is limited, the bottom portion of the header may be eliminated.

stool

2. Measure the height of the door jamb and add 1/4". This should equal the height of the door plus 2". Since a standard residential door is 6'8" high, the rough opening will measure 6'10" <u>from the floor</u> to the under side of the header. Cripples running from the top of the bottom plate to the header would measure 6'8 1/2" long to allow for the 1 1/2 inch thickness of the 2 x 4 bottom plate on which they rest. See (1) above. In actual construction, the door framing studs are installed first, then the cripples are nailed to the door studs at three midway points with 12d nails.

3. The header pieces measure the width of the measured opening plus 3" ... 1 1/2" for the depth of each 2 x 4 cripple upon which they rest. (Refer to the table for recommended header sizes.) The 2 x 4 headers in a non-load-bearing wall are laid flat. In a bearing wall, the 2 x 4 is laid flat and the other members are laid on edge.

Where ceiling clearance is limited, as might be the case in a basement area, and the wall is <u>non</u>-loadbearing, a single 2 x 4 header can be laid flat across the door opening and nailed to the door studs and the flat 2 x 4. Use 12d nails. This type of framing is not as sound and is subject to distortions as temperature and humidity changes occur.

4. Scrap pieces of 2 x 4 cripple are cut and nailed between the header and top plate. Position these to fall in the established sequence of 16" o.c. to assure a good nailing surface for sheathing above the door.

ROUGH FRAMING A WINDOW OPENING

As noted, rough-in stud framing for a window is basically the same as for a door. The standard height from the top of a window is also 6'8", so the steps for determining cripple and header placement are the same as for doors. Because the stool also rests on the cripples, these are cut to length and installed in two pieces on each side.

HEADER SIZING TABLE

Non-loadbearing	up to 48" – 2 x 4
	over 48" – 2 x 6
Bearing	up to 36" – 2 x 4
	36 to 54" – 2 x 6
	54 to 72" – 2 x 8
	over 72" – 2 x 12

The flat 2 x 4 is nailed to the cripples on each end. The other members are nailed to the door studs, the 2 x 4 and to each other. Use 12d nails.

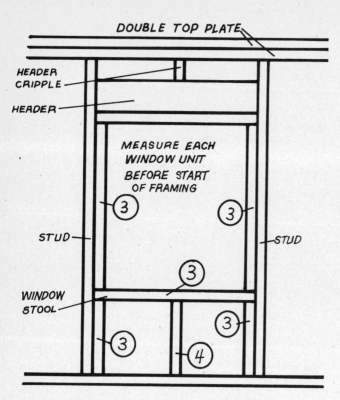

STEPS FOR FRAMING A WINDOW

1. Determine header and cripple location as with door framing.

2. Measure down from the header the height of the window unit plus 1/2" (or window height plus 2") to determine lower header position. Some building codes may require a double lower header.

3. Cut cripples and header to length and install the bottom ones first; then, add the lower header, the upper cripples and install the top header last. Use the chart to select the correct header size for the opening. Nail headers and cripples in place with 12d nails.

4. Add scrap pieces of 2 x 4 between the upper header and top plate at 16" o.c. stud locations. When assembling and nailing door and window framing, make sure the openings are plumb and square. Extra care at this point can save unnecessary trouble and frustrations when installing the prehung units.

WALL CONSTRUCTION METHODS

PREFABRICATION

Walls over ten feet long can be built in shorter sections to facilitate the raising and plumbing before nailing. Prefabricated wall framing is cut 1/4" undersize in height to allow clearance below joists when raising into position. A clearance of 1/4" is also allowed when framing for an obstruction.

When assembling, plates and studs are laid on edge, not flat. Studs are always nailed between plates. Work away from walls and obstruction to allow full-swing hammering.

STEPS TO FOLLOW WHEN PREFABBING A WALL SECTION

1. Measure over-all length of wall sections needed and cut top and bottom plates into convenient and economical lengths. Mark stud locations as explained in "Layout For Basic Wall."

2. Measure existing wall height at several locations. If floor to joist measurements vary, studs will have to be measured and cut individually. If reasonably constant, several studs can be cut together. To determine correct stud length, subtract 3 1/4" from measured wall height where stud will be positioned. This adjusts for the combined thickness of the top and bottom plates and the 1/4" clearance needed for raising the section into position.

3. Cut two end studs to length, set between the plates on edge. Endnail flush with plate ends using two 16d nails into each stud.

END NAILING

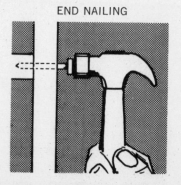

4. Cut 16" o.c. intermediate studs, position and endnail required studs into wall section.

5. Measure ... then double-check each one before cutting and installing headers, cripples and stools for any door and window openings. Read section detailing prehung door and window installation. Do not cut out bottom plate where a door is framed in ... however, saw cut the underside of bottom plate about 1/2" where door frame is located. These cuts are later completed from the top.

6. Raise section into position and secure top plate to joists or rafters with 16d nails.

7. Carefully plumb bottom plate into true vertical position and nail or anchor into position.

8. Repeat the steps for each wall section. Nail abutting sections together with three 12d nails.

REMEMBER ...

Plates and studs are laid on edge - not flat. Studs are always nailed between plates. Work away from walls and obstructions to allow hammering room.

Work in easy-to-handle lengths that can be varied to fit around ducts and other obstructions. If easier, build up to an obstruction and start the next section on the other side. Add required framing for the obstruction.

Be sure a stud is positioned each 16" o.c. to assure a nailing surface when paneling or drywall is added.

DIRECT METHOD

1. Cut top and bottom plates to required length. Lay out and mark each stud position on the plates. To avoid later confusion, mark the right end of both plates and install so they match.

2. Position top plate and nail into place. Use 16d nails.

3. Use a plumbline attached to the end of the top plate and carefully position and secure the bottom plate to the floor. As a double check, move the plumbline to the center of a top plate stud marking and see that it matches the corresponding mark on the bottom plate.

4. Measure the distance between the plates at several locations. If distance varies, measure and cut each stud separately. Otherwise, measure and cut one stud to length and use it as a pattern for cutting the other studs.

5. Position and toenail each stud into the top and bottom plates. H O W recommends the use of three 12d nails - two on one side, one into the center on the other side - at each end of a stud.

Toe or angle nailing.

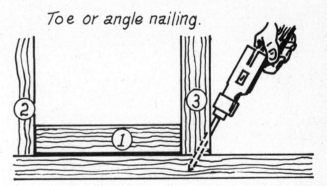

Toenailing may prove difficult for the homeowner unskilled in carpentry. A technique that can simplify and speed up the job is: (1) Cut a 2 x 4 exactly 14 1/2" long. (2) Place it against the first nailed stud. (3) Abutt the next stud up tight against the spacer and toenail to the plate. When the stud is secure, the spacer can be removed with a few hammer taps and placed into position for nailing the next stud. This establishes 16" on-center spacing and prevents the stud from moving off the mark while driving nails into the side. However, the spacer cannot be used between an end stud and the second.

METHODS OF SECURING
TOP PLATES IN PLACE

Whether a wall is built as a direct installation or is prefabricated, it must be tied securely to the house structure. In an existing area, such as a basement, the top plate is secured to the floor joists above.

In an attic area, the top plate is fastened to the roof rafters and the bottom plate to the floor where joists are positioned or to blocking nailed between the joists.

The method used to secure the top plate to the joists above a basement area is determined by the direction the wall is to run ... parallel or perpendicular to the joists.

PARALLEL TO JOISTS

Where possible, a partitioning wall running parallel to joists should be positioned to run between joists.

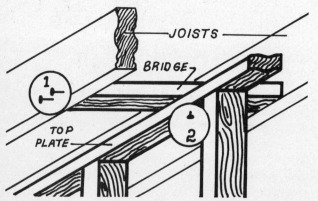

(1) A 2 x 4 bridge or spacer block is cut to length and nailed between two joists. Blocking pieces should be set every 4 ft. and endnailed through the joists.

(2) The top plate is then nailed to the bridging with two 12d nails. Hold the bridge with one hand when nailing into the plate so it does not shift under the hammer blows.

WEAR SAFETY GOGGLES AND ALWAYS
HAVE PLENTY OF LIGHT IN WORK AREA

PERPENDICULAR TO JOISTS

The top plate of a partitioning wall running across or perpendicular to the joists should be nailed at every second or third joist. Using 12d nails, drive through the plate and into the joist.

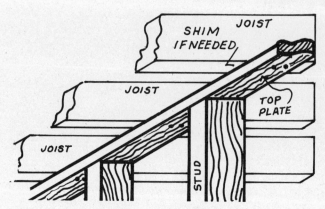

Shims should be inserted to pick up any space between the top plate and joists. Nail through the shims so they are held firmly in place. This will keep a little pressure on the plate and studs and help prevent distortion that could develop as the lumber adjusts to humidity and temperature variations.

SECURING BOTTOM PLATES
TO THE FLOOR

Partition walls on non-masonry floors are simply nailed to the floor with two 12d nails about every 4' along the plate. Some nails should be spaced to catch floor joists. Attachment to masonry floors can be accomplished by three methods--adhesives, masonry nails or anchor bolts.

Adhesives come in cartridges and are used with a hand-operated caulking gun. Select a quality masonry adhesive and follow the manufacturer's directions to the letter. Drive two or more concrete nails to hold plate in position while the glue sets up. The key is making certain the surface is clean and free of powdery cement.

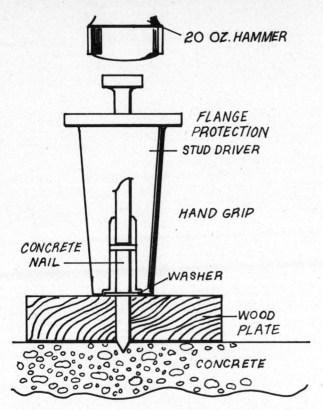

20 OZ. HAMMER

FLANGE PROTECTION

STUD DRIVER

HAND GRIP

CONCRETE NAIL

WASHER

WOOD PLATE

CONCRETE

Masonry nails are of specially
hardened steel. They can be
driven into concrete with a hammer. This is relatively slow
and noisy work. H O W recommends an inexpensive holding and
driving tool called a stud driver
used with a 20 oz. hammer having
a convex-shaped head. The stud
driver holds the nail. A protective flange near the top shields
the holding hand while driving
the nail. Concrete nails should
be embedded at least 1" into the
masonry. Use a 2 1/2" or 3" nail
to secure bottom plates, set at
each end of a wall and every 24"
to 36" along the plate. Wear
safety goggles and hearing pro-
tectors!

Another more expensive method is
with a power stud gun which uses
blank 22 or 32 caliber cartridges
to "shoot" a special type nail
into the bottom plate and the masonry. There is a potential dan-
ger when shooting nails so follow
operating instructions carefully.
Power stud guns can be rented.
Know the linear run of bottom
plates so the correct number of
shot and nails can be determined.

Anchor bolts take the most time
to install but are the strongest
type of attachment, and can be
used in conjunction with other
methods. They consist of two
parts - the bolt and its matching
lead anchor. A hole is drilled
in the concrete to receive the
anchor. A hole through the plate
permits the bolt to be screwed
into the anchor. A 1/4" x 3"
bolt should be set every 4' to 6'
along the length with at least
two per plate.

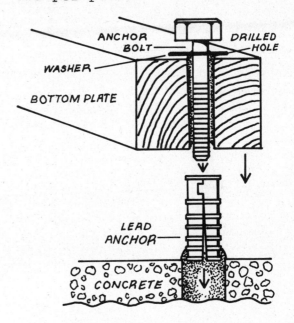

ANCHOR BOLT

DRILLED HOLE

WASHER

BOTTOM PLATE

LEAD ANCHOR

CONCRETE

INSTALLING ANCHOR BOLTS

1. Mark and drill holes in bottom
plate for bolts. The drill bit
diameter should match the bolt and
anchor selected.

2. Position the bottom plate pre-
cisely where it is to be secured.
Put a heavy nail into each pre-
drilled hole along the plate and
hit it hard enough to scar or
chip the masonry.

CAUTION: ON DIRECT INSTALLATION,
MAKE SURE BOLT HOLES ARE NOT
DRILLED WHERE 16" O.C. STUDS WILL
FALL.

USE A DRILL STOP ON THE BIT ADJUSTED TO THE LENGTH OF THE ANCHOR

CONCRETE

3. Move the plate out of the way and drill anchor bolt holes at each mark ... using a masonry bit turning at a slow speed in a variable speed electric drill. The bit should match the diameter of the lead anchor and the hole should be deep enough so no part of the anchor protrudes above the concrete floor when inserted.

In prefab walls, anchor bolt holes can be located and drilled by nailing the top plate into position, scarring the masonry, and then swinging the base of the wall away a few inches to allow drilling of the holes.

4. Insert lead anchor. Position the bottom plate and insert bolt through the plate and into its anchor. Tighten bolt against bottom plate.

TEN REMINDERS FOR A BETTER JOB

1. Perfectly straight studs are a rarity but select the straightest for top and bottom plates by sighting along the narrow side. Next best are used for door and window framing, then studs. Where a borderline stud must be used, it will pay to nail 2 x 4 spacer blocks between the two adjacent studs to prevent further distortion. Badly warped or twisted lengths can be cut and used for blocking and bracing.

2. Before nailing studs to the top and bottom plates on a direct-type installation, use a level to plumb each stud into final position.

3. Framing along an exterior wall of a basement can sometimes pose this problem: A space usually is found between the top of the foundation wall and the floor joists. A sill plate is secured to the top of the foundation and the joists actually rest on this plate. A 2" x 2" can be forced into the recess and nailed to become a flush nailing surface for top plates, ceiling furring strips or wall angle.

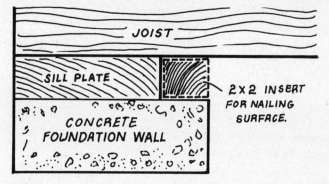

JOIST

SILL PLATE

2 x 2 INSERT FOR NAILING SURFACE.

CONCRETE FOUNDATION WALL

4. Where a fairly long partitioning wall will run parallel to the joists, position it to run between joists by adding blocking. A short wall length can run directly under and be fastened to a joist.

5. The bridging ("X" bracing) between floor joists should not be permanently removed. These hold joists in position. Check all bridging for tightness. In time, nails can work loose. Drive them tight again.

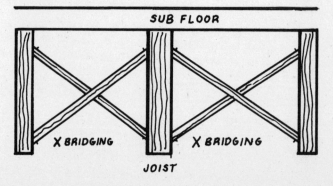

SUB FLOOR

X BRIDGING   X BRIDGING

JOIST

If a flush ceiling is to be installed, some of the bridging
ends may hang below the joist
edges. Remove that briding
piece, saw off 1/4" to 1/2" in a
mitre box and reinstall. This
is not required with a suspended
ceiling system because the ceiling grids are suspended by wires
below joist level.

6. A stud wall can be framed with
2 x 2's, 2 x 4's, 2 x 6's or larger. Where space is needed for
plumbing drain lines, use 2 x 6
studs or offset a regular 2 x 4
stud wall from the existing wall
to permit running the necessary
pipes in the space. In areas
where temperatures drop below
freezing for any prolonged period
water lines running near any outside wall should be properly
insulated.

7. Concrete floors, whether basement or garage, are seldom level;
the clearance from floor to joist
can vary along a proposed wall
line. Take several measurements
between the floor and joists to
determine the variations in stud
lengths. There is generally a
noticeable floor slope from a
perimeter wall to a floor drain;

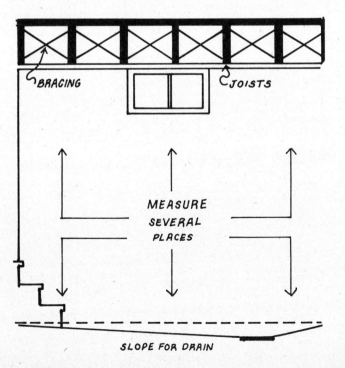

BRACING   JOISTS

MEASURE
SEVERAL
PLACES

SLOPE FOR DRAIN

therefore, take a number of measurements when constructing a
partitioning wall that cuts
across this natural slope to a
drain. Shim plates where needed.

8. Adequate insulation and an effective vapor barrier is necessary where exterior concrete
walls or masonry floors are to be
enclosed. Review Insulation
section.

In the case of floors, a polyethylene film is stapled to the
top of the furring strips before
the underlayment is installed.

9. All doors or openings should
be wide enough for easy clearance
of furniture, appliances and
other large units. Outside doors
and entries to laundry and furnace areas should have 36" openings. Others should be at least
30" wide. Pre-hung doors are
available in any standard size.

If swing room for a door is restricted by overhead obstructions, permanent objects or planned location of furniture, consider using sliding or folding
type doors.

10. Open top or half walls are effective room dividers. They can
be made any length, usually 4" to
8" wide. The 4" wide divider wall
should be considered only if it
will have vertical support at each
end, such as an existing wall at
one end and a column to the ceiling at the other The vertical
support is needed to prevent wobble. The 8" wide divider wall
does not need both vertical supports if properly anchored. It
is constructed as a double wall,
i.e., two identical 2 x 4 wall
sections tied together. It should
be solidly anchored to the floor
and the nails or anchor bolts
should be set 1" from the outside
edge of the plate at each end and
every 36" along the wall length.

CARPENTRY

FINISH

Everything accomplished up to this point now begins to pay off! Behind-the-scenes construction work that gives size and shape to the area has been framed in. The next phase is adding wall, ceiling and floor covering to enclose it. Good planning and careful workmanship will produce that "professional" look, so read this chapter and the one on planning before starting to move ahead.

DRYWALL (GYPSUM BOARD)

For drywall installations, the sheathing material used is gypsum board. It is a paper-covered 4' x 8' sheet of gypsum plaster that has slightly tapered edges where sheets abut. A special moisture resistant surface is available for use in bathrooms and other high humidity areas.

Perhaps the most reassuring feature of drywall is that reasonable mistakes in cutting and fit-

ting can be corrected easily. Cracks, dents and joints are taped and filled ... molding and baseboard can hide a multitude of errors and corner bead corrects outside corner abutments.

The simplest way to cut drywall board is with a sharp utility knife and a straight-edge. Transfer measurements to the lighter and smoother finish side, marking at several points. Hold the straight-edge firmly in place and score through the paper and into the plaster core. Make sure the cut is equally as deep on the outside edges as in the middle.

To complete the break, strike the back side of the panel at the cut point with the heel of the hand. This will complete the break in the core plaster and by bending one end back about 45 degrees, a crease will be evident. Use the utility knife to cut through the back paper cover. If the cut is

```
┌─────────────────────────────────────────────────────────────────────┐
│              TOOLS NEEDED        Annular-ringed nails ... approxi-    │
│                                  mately 1/2 lb. per 100 sq. ft. of    │
│   Utility knife w/replaceable blade   drywall.  Use 1 1/4" for panels│
│                                  up to 1/2" thick; a 1 3/8" is        │
│   Keyhole saw                    needed for 5/8" thickness.           │
│                                                                       │
│   4 ft. long board with straight edge  Pre-mixed ... or dry-mixed joint│
│                                  compound with two 5-gal con-         │
│   Measuring tape                 tainers and mixing paddle.           │
│                                                                       │
│   Heavy lead pencil              Joint reinforcing tape               │
│                                                                       │
│   Hammer pref. with convex head  Corner bead, if required            │
│                                                                       │
│   Standard or aviation-type metal  Open-grit sandpaper and wood-      │
│   shears                         sanding block                        │
│                                                                       │
│   Finishing knives - one 6" wide  Bread or baking pan to hold con-    │
│                      one 10" wide  venient working amounts of joint   │
│              MATERIALS NEEDED    compound.                            │
│                                                                       │
│   Required number of Gypsum panels                                    │
├─────────────────────────────────────────────────────────────────────┤
│   Note:  In estimating amount of pre-mix required, figure one gallon for│
│   first 100 square feet and one more for each additional 200 square feet│
│   of drywall to be installed.                                         │
│   With dry mix, about 6 pounds per 100 square feet should be ordered. │
│   When mixing, sift powder through fingers into water, letting powdered│
│   compound absorb the water.  It is best not to stir, as this speeds up│
│   the setting-up process and thereby reduces working time.            │
└─────────────────────────────────────────────────────────────────────┘
```

jagged, smooth out the edge, using the knife blade or coarse sandpaper over a hand-size block of wood. Perfect cuts are not necessary but the better they are will help the job go faster since less time will be spent patching, filling and taping.

Holes for switches and receptacles are made by punching the tip of a keyhole saw through the center of the area to be removed and then cutting to shape and size. Be careful ... fixture plates must cover the cutouts completely.

Where gypsum board is installed merely as an underlayment for another surfacing material, such as paneling, it should be properly nailed, but taping and filling are not necessary. When it will be the finished surface of the wall and only paint or wallpaper will be applied as the final covering, finishing procedures must be completed.

NAILING DRYWALL (GYPSUM BOARD)

If both ceiling and walls are to be finished in drywall, the ceiling should be installed first. If working alone, build a pair of tees to hold full sheets against the joists while nailing. Even 1/2" material in 4 x 8 ft. sheets is heavy and 5/8's can really try the muscles and patience of the person tackling the work for the first time. An extra pair of hands is recommended.

NOT LESS THAN 3/8" IN FROM EDGE.

**7" ON CEILINGS
8" ON WALLS**

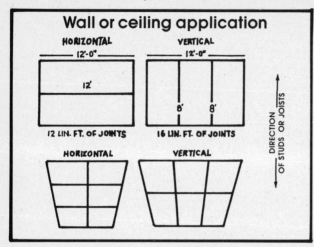

Make a T-brace with a 2-ft. length of 1 x 4 nailed to a 2 x 4 upright that is 1/2" longer than floor-to-ceiling height. Wedge the T-brace between floor and panel to support panel ends while nailing. Keep firm contact with joists.

T-BRACE

When positioning drywall sheets, leave a gap the width of a dime between all joints to allow compound to penetrate and adhere to the interior layer of plaster core. Space nails no more than 7" apart on ceilings ... 8" on walls. Set the nails in from the edge about 3/8 inch or enough to prevent splitting the drywall edge while getting a good bite on the framing member. Hold panel firmly against framing and nail the center of the panel first, perimeters last. Dimple nailheads for filling with joint compound. Do not overdrive or countersink nails. This will break the paper or fracture the plaster.

However, if the dimple is too shallow, age, stress and vibration can loosen the drywall nails and the filled area will pop out exposing the nailhead. Experience on a panel or two is all that is needed. A crown head carpenter's hammer works fine.

A new design drywall nail is available. The underside of the head is shaped liked a flathead screw and this gradual slope permits driving the head flush with the surface. The top of the head is concave and receives and holds the fill compound. The board surface does not have to be dimpled. These improvements over the standard drywall nail should be helpful to the non-professional.

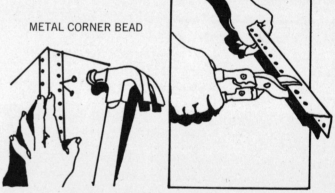

METAL CORNER BEAD

Drive nails side by side on adjoining sheets to minimize seam cracking later. Perforated drywall tape is used to finish all seams, inside corners and large cracks. Corner beading should be installed on all outside corners for both the added strength and appearance. Use a snip to cut metal corner bead to exact length. Cut through each flange first, then bend or cut if using aviation shears. When nailing corner bead in place, hold it firmly to the corner and nail through the small holes on each flange. Space about 9" and make sure the nails are driven tightly into framing members.

46

STEPS FOR FILLING AND TAPING

1. Joint compound is available in an unmixed dry form or ready-to-use cans. If mixing, follow the directions on the package and make up only the amount needed to first coat seams, patches and nailheads.

A medium consistency mixture is applied to each seam and nail dent. Use a 6" wide flexible taping knife. Center perforated drywall tape over seams and large cracks. Use the taping tool to squeeze out air bubbles and excess cement. Hold the top of the tape in place while drawing the knife firmly along the tape. Use enough compound to embed tape under a thin layer to fill tapered edges. Allow to dry about 24 hours.

To finish end joints which are not wrapped with paper, apply the compound and center the tape over the joint. Do not overlap tape when it is applied at tapered joints.

Before filling nail dents, draw the taping knife blade over the heads. If it "clicks" against the head, hammer it in further. Then fill all dimples and dents with compound ... apply in a sweeping motion in one direction. Take the excess off by sweeping the blade in the opposite direction. It should be level with the surface of the panel. These also should dry thoroughly before applying the next coat.

2. Sand lightly before applying the second coat. Use a slightly thinner mixture of joint compound to cover the tape and nail patches again. Use a 10" or 12" knife or trowel to level this coat evenly. Extend coverage about 2" beyond taping coat. Feather both edges by putting a little extra pressure on the knife edge as it is drawn across each patch and along the seams. This coat should dry 24 hours.

USE A WIDE BLADE KNIFE

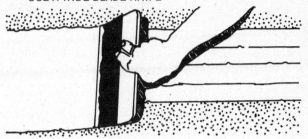

3. A final coat of compound is applied to completely hide the tape. This is feathered out at least 6" on each side. After this has dried thoroughly, all filled surfaces should be sanded with a medium sandpaper until the tape and patches blend in with the drywall. All tape edges should be feathered so they are not visible. The better the sanding job, the better appearance the wall will have when painted or papered. Wipe plaster dust away with a damp cloth.

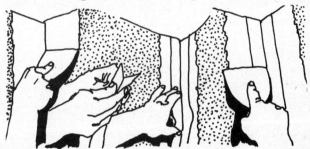

4. For inside corners, use the 6" knife to "butter" compound 3" on both sides of the corner and into the crack. Fold the tape strip along the center crease and lightly press into the corner. Press the edges into the compound with the finishing knife. Gently press the seam into the corner. Hold at the top and draw knife along both sides to remove excess compound.

After the 24-hour drying time, apply the second coat ... ONE SIDE AT A TIME ... allowing the first to set up before doing the second. This procedure helps prevent "scarring" the opposite corner with the knife. Feather out beyond the first coat. The third and final coat follows the steps above.

5. Outside corners are filled a little differently. Use the 6" knife to lay in enough compound on the flanges to fill from the bead out beyond the flanges. Don't try to do a long length ... about 2 ft. is best.

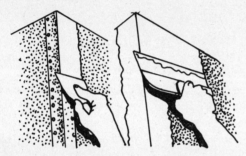

Level the compound by letting one edge of the knife slide on the nose bead while the other tracks outside the flange. Feather out about 4" on each side. After drying, repeat steps 2 and 3.

6. Check for small nicks or dents that were missed. Fill with joint cement, sand smooth when dry. NOTE: A LIGHT-COLORED WALL REVEALS FEWER IMPERFECTIONS. A DARKER COLOR TENDS TO EXAGGERATE THEM.

PRECAUTIONS ... SUGGESTIONS

1. When sanding tape seams and patches, use an opencoat fine sandpaper. Wrap around a hand-size block of wood, apply light pressure. DO NOT USE COARSE PAPER OR ANY TYPE OF POWER SANDER.

2. Wet-sanding or wiping smooth with a sponge is sometimes recommended rather than dry-sanding. Plaster dust is particulary fine; can stay suspended in the room atmosphere for considerable time. Ventilate, wear goggles and a nose and mouth mask or respirator to protect both eyes and lungs.

If a sand-based paint is to be used for the drywall surface, the final sanding of taped cracks and joints and nailing dents is less critical because many of the imperfections will be hidden by the rougher finish induced by the sand.

REPAIRING DRYWALL DAMAGE

Drywall damage, whether crushed, dented or punctured, is easily repaired to look like new. A common damage occurs when a door knob repeatedly strikes an unprotected wall. Sometimes an area below a window becomes soft and puffy from wetness.

1. The first step in making a professional-looking repair is to cut out the damaged portion. Determine the true size of the damaged area by examining the surrounding area for surface cracks and breaks. Mark a square or rectangle encompassing the damaged area and remove with a sharp utility knife. A keyhole saw can be used but extreme care should be taken not to cut into pipes or electrical wires within the wall.

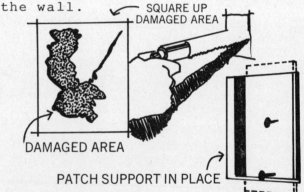

2. The next step is to make a backing support for the drywall patch. This can be made from a scrap piece of drywall or thin piece of wood. Cut the patch support about one inch narrower and two to four inches longer than the opening. Drive a nail (8d or larger) through the patch support in such a way that when the patch support is in position the nail rests on the bottom of the enlarged opening.

Put another nail through the center of the patch support. Then pull it out and string a 6" piece of wire or string through the hole. On the backside wrap or tie the end around a match stick, washer or other retainer. The lead out the front side is used to hold the support patch firmly in place while it dries.

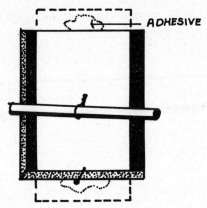

3. Apply joint cement or adhesive to the long ends of the patch support. Work it into the opening and adjust so the center is behind the opening and the nail rests on the bottom of the opening. Pull it up tight and roll the string or wire around the strip of wood that is wider than the hole. Allow 12 hours for the compound or adhesive to dry.

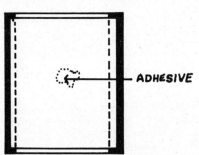

4. The critical step is patching the opening. Cut a patch to size from drywall of the <u>same thickness</u> as that used in the existing wall. Allow about 1/8" clearance all around the patch for joint compound bonding. Pull out the bottom nail support and cut off the wire or string tie flush. Apply a small amount of joint compound to the back of the patch and set it in position. Tape and finish the patch as detailed.

DO'S AND DON'TS

DO--mix casein-based compounds to a heavy consistency. Add necessary additional water after soaking for required consistency.

DO--add powdered compounds to water when mixing--not water to powder. And sift compounds while pouring.

DO--keep tools and mixing containers clean at all times. Always use clean water for mixing.

DO--apply compounds of heavy consistency over fastener heads.

DO--apply three coats for finest results.

DO--apply relatively thin coats in corners to prevent cracking.

DO--minimize fill coat craters by applying the finish coat with firm pressure and with tool held at 45 degree.

DO--fill 1/4" or wider open joints and allow to dry before proceeding with regular joint finishing.

DON'T--build crowns over joints. This will produce shadow areas.

DON'T--combine casein-based compounds with any non-casein-based compound.

DON'T--combine powdered and ready-mixed compounds.

DON'T--apply excess knife pressure when spotting nailheads. This practice scoops compound out of the dimpled area surrounding the fastener.

DON'T--paint before joints are thoroughly dry. Painting wet joints causes discloration.

DON'T--overthin compounds with water. Excess water can cause delayed shrinkage and bond failures.

INSTALLING NEW SHEATHING OVER EXISTING CEILING AND WALLS

Sometimes neglect or simply age and repeated papering and painting can result in cracked, peeling walls and ceiling. The solution may be to strip down to bare walls but these, too, may be in bad shape. Recovering existing walls with drywall can be accomplished at reasonable expense and quickly bring the room up to the point of decorating. These eight steps explain how:

1. Carefully remove all door, window, cove, baseboard and base shoe trim and moldings. Remove heating grills, wall receptacles, switches and cover plates <u>after</u> the circuit for the room has been disconnected at the panel. To be certain each circuit is "cold," use a circuit tester; take all necessary precautions including testing the tester first in an outlet known to be "hot." If ceilings are to be resurfaced, test, then remove light fixture. Tape each wire end and tuck back into its box. Cut away old sheathing around each electrical box to allow pulling the nail and moving the box forward approximately 1/2" or the amount that equals the thickness of the sheathing to be used in covering the old surface.

2. At this point, additional wall outlets can be installed. Cut away enough old wall sheathing to run new wiring to each new outlet location desired. THIS MUST BE IN ACCORDANCE WITH LOCAL CODES.

3. Nail #1 pine screen molding on edges of all door and window jambs. This molding should be 3/4" wide by the thickness of the wall sheathing to be added. This will bring the jambs flush with the new wall surface.

4. Locate stud positions behind old wall. Mark on the floor and ceiling as a nailing guide for the new sheathing. If ceiling

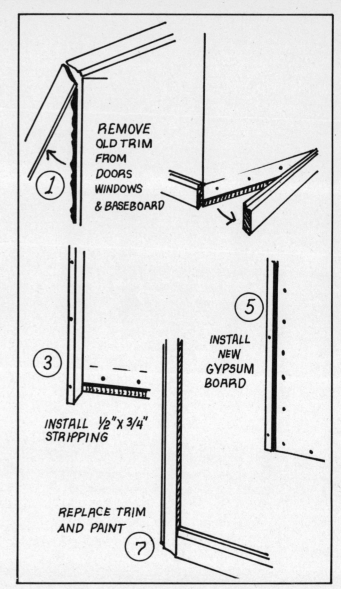

is being resurfaced, it should be completed first. Locate joists and mark positions.

5. Install new paneling, drywall or other material. Tape and sand if drywall is used.

6. Reinstall old door and window trim--or replace with new trim.

7. Reinstall old baseboard, base shoe or replace with new pieces. Install cove molding at wall/ceiling joint if desired.

8. Reinstall all electrical switches, outlets, light fixtures and cover plates. If the devices are old or worn, replace with new elements. Remount heating duct grills.

INSTALLING PANEL

The growing popularity of paneling as a wall finish has spurred
the creation of a wide range of
patterns and materials by manufacturers. Today, there is paneling to fit just about any purpose
or personal taste. The ultimate
selection is only restricted by
the dollars available to achieve
the desired "look." Most panels
measure 4' x 8' to match standard
stud placement; however, some are
available in longer lengths ...
up to 12 feet.

For general purposes, paneling
falls into three categories:

1. HARDBOARD - natural wood veneer

2. PARTICLE BOARD   - manufactured
from wood particles with the
printed facing laminated to the
particle board

3. PLYWOOD

All have a wood base and are
therefore subject to physical
change due to temperature and humidity. It is recommended that
paneling be stored for 72 hours
in the room where it is to be installed to permit adjustment to
room conditions.

Wood paneling is cut and fashion-
ed with standard carpentry tools:

1. Fine-tooth cross cut or combination hand saw, sabre saw or
power circular saw with plywood
blade. It is IMPORTANT to remember that the panel be FACE UP
when using a <u>hand</u> <u>saw</u> ... FACE
DOWN when using <u>any</u> <u>power</u> <u>saw</u>.
The reason for this caution:
<u>Power</u> <u>saws</u> cut on the <u>up</u> stroke
and this can cause splintering
along the cut when the face of
the panel is up.

TAPE MARK PANEL

An alternative is to lay masking
tape along the path of proposed
cuts. Then measure and mark the
line of cut, making sure it
falls on the tape. Saw through
the tape and panel along the
marks.

A fine-toothed keyhole saw is
needed for cutting electrical
outlet holes if a sabre saw is
not available.

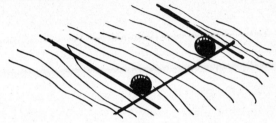

2. A power drill or brace with a
bit large enough to make starting
holes for the keyhole saw. With
practice, a sabre saw canted well
forward can also make a starting
hole.

3. Hammer and nails ... either 3d
finishing or special nails with
heads color coated to match the
color tones of the paneling. If
not color coated, a putty stick
of matching color is available.

4. Nail set with the point the
size of the head of finishing
nail used.

5. Level - 24" is suggested for
accuracy.

6. Chalk line - <u>chalked</u>

7. Short shims of various thickness to raise panels off the
floor for squaring to the abutting panel.

8. If using adhesive, a caulking
gun and sufficient tubes of
panel adhesive to complete the
job. Be sure the adhesive is a
moisture-proof type.

If walls are waterproofed, test
a small area to see if adhesive
is compatible with waterproofing.
Do not use over asphaltic or

silicone waterproofing. Do not
apply over wallpaper. Do not apply hardboard paneling directly
to brick, concrete or block walls.

Preparation - All contact surfaces must be firm, hard, clean
and dry--free of dirt, grease,
oil and all foreign matter. Store
sheathing panels and adhesive at
approximately 70º F. 24 hours
prior to use.

Applying to framing members - Cut
and fit panel as needed including
cut-outs for wall outlets. Use
cartridge in caulking gun. Cut
plastic nozzle tip of cartridge
on slant to allow 1/8" or 1/4"
bead. Puncture inner seal at
base of tip with long nail. Apply
1/8" to 1/4" adhesive bead to
framing member. Bead may be continuous or in broken lines of 3"
bead and 3" skip. Where two
panels butt, a serpentine bead
should be applied to the stud. If
framing member is not straight or
panel is warped, apply adhesive
in sufficient quantity in hollows
to even the surface.

Application to solid backing -
Apply continuous bead 1" from
each edge of panel and two continuous or interrupted beads on
16" spans between the edges of
the panels (4 beads per panel).

Setting panels - Before installing panel ... wait for adhesive
to develop quick grab, follow
manufacturer's instructions
exactly. Set panel into position and press firmly into place.
Panel may be anchored at top and
bottom with 3 or 4 brads or use
blocks on floor to hold panel
snug. Adjustments can usually be
made for 20 or 30 minutes after
positioning. Tap panel with rubber mallet or padded hammer over
entire bonding surface to insure
contact. Repeat tapping procedure after panels have remained
in position for 45 minutes to one
hour. Tools and smears should be
cleaned with solvent recommended
by manufacturer.

PREPARATION

NEW STUDWALL FRAMING

If the studs are seasoned and
fairly straight, nail 2 x 4 blocks
between studs about halfway between the floor and ceiling. The
panel sheets are then nailed or
bonded with panel adhesive directly to the studs.

Sometimes the stud wall is out of
plumb, studs are not correctly
spaced for panel edges to meet at
the stud centers. In this case,
1" x 3" furring strips will have
to be installed and extra studs
nailed into the existing wall
frame where necessary to provide
a nailing surface at each 16"
center.

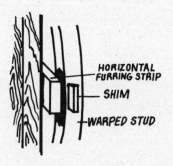

HORIZONTAL FURRING STRIP
SHIM
WARPED STUD

When furring, nail horizontal
strips 16" on center from floor
to ceiling. A vertical strip is
secured at each 4' interval where
panel edges will meet. Shim out
furring with wood shingle wher-
ever necessary to assure a solid
supporting surface ... otherwise,
panels will acquire a noticeably
wavy appearance.

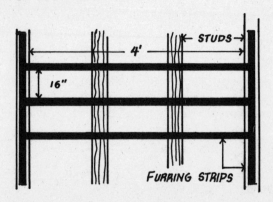

STUDS
4'
16"
FURRING STRIPS

EXISTING WALL SURFACES

Remove all door and window trim, baseboard and cove molding as explained under Drywall.

To locate existing studs, try one of the following:

1. One or more studs may be visible where the old wall and floor meet. If necessary, cut or chip away a small portion of the wall surface material near the floor ... where the first stud should fall. Measure and mark along wall each 16" on center position of succeeding studs, marking each in chalk on the floor and ceiling as a future nailing guide.

2. Measure from a corner approximately 12 3/4" ... gently tap a thin finishing nail into the wall surface near the floor to locate the first stud off the corner. If not "hit" the first time, try 1/2" on either side of first test point. If still no contact, make same test on other side of the corner ... the carpenter may have been left-handed and built the wall counter-clockwise.

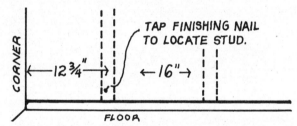

TAP FINISHING NAIL TO LOCATE STUD.

CORNER

← 12¾" → ← 16" →

FLOOR

If existing walls are badly cracked, have a rough textured finish or noticeable hollows, install furring strips as previously explained.

Concrete, masonry or stone walls should be thoroughly waterproofed before any sheathing is applied. If the existing walls are painted and that paint is in good condition with no peeling or flaking, the chances are it has been waterproofed. If any moisture problem is evident, use a top quality sealant to correct the situation before furring or installing a

stud wall frame. Follow the manufacturer's instruction carefully.

Furring strips can be nailed or glued together to form a frame similar to a standard stud wall ... then fastened into place with masonry nails (hard work), lead anchors or a moisture-proof adhesive plus a few holding nails.

INSTALLING PANEL SECTIONS

When fitting panels into place, DO NOT force the fit. Allow at least 1/32" space between panels. Thin nails (3d or 4d) can be lightly tacked 12" from the top and bottom next to the edge of the first panel installed to maintain the necessary spacing. Remove tacks as adjoining panel is secured. Repeat along the wall. When completed, it should be possible to slip a dime between each panel from top to bottom.

Always nail from the center of the panel to the edges--NEVER BOTH EDGES AND THEN THE MIDDLE! Recess nail heads just enough to allow covering with color matching putty stick. Butt panels for outside corners and cover with outside corner molding. Butt panels for inside corners, then install inside corner moldings.

A variety of special mastics are made that will hold a panel firmly in place and eliminate the nailing and filling procedure described. The properties of these mastics vary somewhat; therefore, follow the directions of the manufacturer. When installing to studs or furring strips, apply the adhesive to the lumber rather than the panel. Use a few finishing nails to hold the panel in place while the glue sets up ... then remove. Proper glueing technique is to use enough for the job but no more than enough. Maintain the 1/32" spacing be-

tween abutting panels as with
nailing.

If installing directly to concrete or existing walls, a 1/4"
bead of adhesive is applied to
the back of the panel. Keep
about 1/2" from the outer edges
so the glue will not "squish" out
between abutting panels. Apply
where cross blocking occurs, too.
For added rigidity and insulation
3/8" drywall can be nailed to the
studs first with the long side
running with the wall (see Drywall). The paneling is then
glued or nailed to the surface.
The drywall does not require fill
ing and taping.

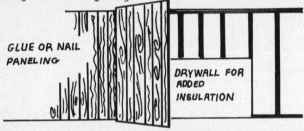

GLUE OR NAIL
PANELING

DRYWALL FOR
ADDED
INSULATION

ELECTRICAL OUTLETS

Cutouts for receptacles and
switches must be accurate and
clearly positioned on the back
of affected panels. Do this
carefully ... it is the cause of
many ruined pieces of expensive
4 x 8 sheets. Chalk edges of
outlet boxes and correctly position the panel in front of the
chalked box. Strike face of
panel sharply several times with
heel of hand to transfer outline
of box to back of panel. A hole
is drilled in the center of the
area outlined and a fine-toothed
keyhole or sabre saw is used to
cut the marked opening.

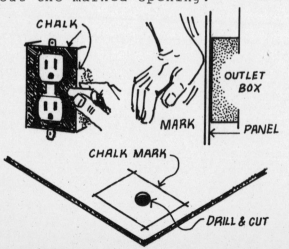

CHALK

OUTLET
BOX

MARK

PANEL

CHALK MARK

DRILL & CUT

FITTING DOORS AND WINDOWS

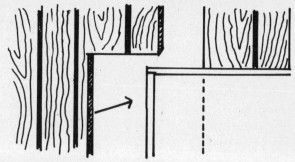

Cut paneling to fit. Try to have
the groove sequence match the
preceding full panel. Trim with
matching prefinished molding.
When paneling old walls, rabbet
(groove) old casing with a router so it fits flush with the
paneling. Refinish with stain
to match.

An alternative method: Fur out
the area from which trim was removed with thin strips the same
thickness as the paneling to be
used.

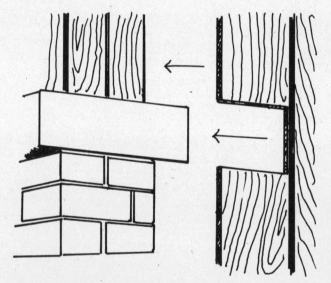

To fit paneling against a fireplace, bricks, stones or other
irregular abutments, make a template. Push a long strip of
kraft paper against the uneven
surface and trace the outline.
Cut out the resulting shape and
test it in position. Adjust
where required. Then transfer
the outline to the panel face
using chalk or water soluble
crayon. Cut out shape with a
coping saw. Install and fill in
cracks with putty stick.

CERAMIC TILE

Potentially damp or wet areas such as shower and tub enclosures, kitchen and bathroom counters and laundry areas should have surfaces which resist or actually repel moisture. The most popular and durable of these is ceramic tile. It is readily available in two forms: 12 x 12 inch mesh square covered with 1 x 1 or 1 x 2 inch tile pieces spaced properly for grouting ... or individual 4" square tiles with built-in flanges to aid in maintaining even spacing on four sides.

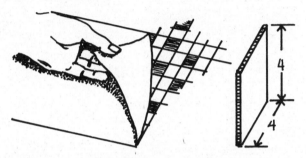

Tools required are minimal: a toothed spreader for the mastic ... a tile nipper for the sheet type tiles or a sharp glass cutter for the 4" square type. In addition, a chalk line and level are needed to establish true horizontal and vertical starting lines. Remember, even newly constructed walls are rarely square, so be sure the starting line represents true vertical and horizontal.

The tile nipper enables the home-owner to cut and fashion the small squares to fit around pipes and fixtures. The large square tile pieces are cut like pane glass ... a line is scored with the cutter wheel along a straight edge and then snapped along a board or table edge. Some like to use a heavy wire coat hanger, placing the scored line over the wire and hitting the tile smartly with the heel of the hand.

Just like any other finishing project, the first three steps call for:

1. Accurate measuring.

2. The purchase of sufficient materials and necessary tools.

3. Preparation of the surface to the degree needed to assure a good end result.

The first decision, especially for a shower/tub enclosure is whether the tiled surface will run to the ceiling or just part way up. A partial wall should be at least as high as the shower head. Use the chalk line and level to establish the top line of tile. If in a tub enclosure, measure down from this line at three points on the wall to establish a true horizontal above the tub ... other times, a number of tiles will have to be cut to fit the space. NEVER START AT THE TUB ... start at the top mark so this line appears level with the top of the wall.

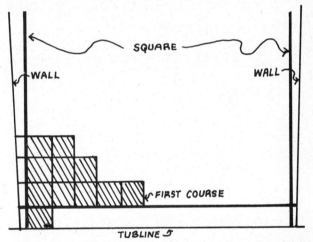

Cover a section of the area to be tiled with ceramic tile adhesive, using manufacturer's recommendations for spreader and notch size and the amount of adhesive. Do not cover more wall surface than you can easily tile before the adhesive sets up.

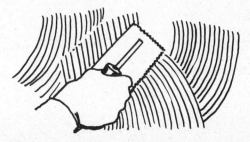

55

Apply the ceramic tile one row at a time. Continue with the next rows of tile until the desired height is reached. After tile is applied, let it cure overnight.

When applying grout, use a squeegee or your bare hands. Force grout deep into each tile joint and press firmly to eliminate air pockets. Wipe away excess with a wet sponge, then let grout set up about one hour. Dampen sponge and smooth the grouted cracks, wipe away the powdery film from the tile surface.

Allow the grout to cure several days. Then, a sealer such as silicone can be sprayed on to increase water resistance and help retard staining or discoloration of the grout.

SETTING A PRE-HUNG DOOR

Pre-hung doors are delivered with bands and temporary nailing to hold everything in place. A small cardboard spacer is between the door and jamb. Trim is included ... consisting of six pieces, two short and four long, for trimming out the top and sides of a doorway on each side of the wall.

Doors are available in various natural woods, and lumber yards carry the more popular ones in stock. Mahogany is popular because of lower cost. Birch, ash, beech and walnut cost proportionately more. Most interior doors made today are hollow core. Solid doors, unless made to order, are usually found in colonial or louvred styles. Trim is white pine unless another kind of wood is special ordered.

1. DO NOT remove any bands or nails. Set the door gently in place in order to "eyeball" the general fit with the framed opening. Check particularly for warped studs and whether there is a severe floor slope running with the wall. Check the plumb of the wall frame. If floor slope tends to throw the door out of plumb, it may be necessary to shorten the vertical door jamb on the <u>high side</u> to compensate.

2. Remove split jamb section and set HINGED SIDE of jamb against framing stud. Tack lightly, using two or three #4 finishing nails. Leave the heads protruding enough to permit easy withdrawal with claw hammer. Set shims between frame studs and jamb until hinged side is plumb and square.

3. Bring LATCH side of door into alignment with wall facing and tack lightly as in Step 2. Drive shim between frame studs and jamb as before. CAUTION: Do not shim too tightly. Allow 1/8" clearance between door and jamb to permit door to swing freely with no binding. Check alignment: the latch side must be plumb and square, too.

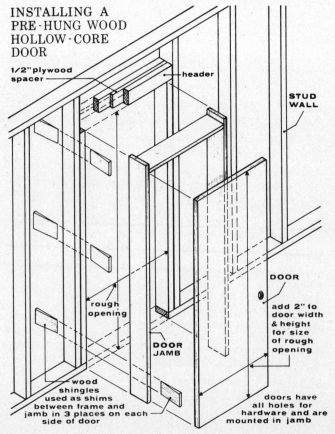

INSTALLING A PRE-HUNG WOOD HOLLOW-CORE DOOR

1/2" plywood spacer

header

STUD WALL

rough opening

DOOR

add 2" to door width & height for size of rough opening

DOOR JAMB

wood shingles used as shims between frame and jamb in 3 places on each side of door

doors have all holes for hardware and are mounted in jamb

4. Remove all spacers, bands, etc.; open and close the door several times to determine where shims should be added to bring jamb into true alignment. When adding shims, be sure they do not create excessive pressure on the jamb as this could restrict door movement.

5. Proceed to nail jamb securely to the frame studs on both hinged and latch sides. MAKE CERTAIN ALL NAILS GO THROUGH A SHIM AND NOT DIRECTLY FROM JAMB TO STUD! Use two #8 finishing nails, one on each side of the door stop, in about three or four places from top to bottom. Check the alignment periodically by opening and closing the door several times as nailing proceeds.

The thing to watch for in final nailing is that the final hammer blows are not compressing the shims enough to throw jamb out of square. This is the principal reason why nails should only be driven where a shim has been inserted. If only a few shims are necessary to bring the jamb into true alignment, add more where nailing. Be sure these extra shims are just thick enough to fill the space without putting pressure against the jamb.

6. Recess all nail heads with nailset. Exercise care that hammer does not strike the wood facing and make a dent. If door has split jamb, install the second section to match sheathing on other side of wall. Nail in place. Secure to jamb and frame with three #4 nails on each side.

TRIM A DOOR

Follow these steps to trim an existing or new door.

1. Look at the door trim on the doors in the house; notice how it was fitted and nailed. For doors, start with the short pieces at the top of the frame. With modern or colonial standard trim, use 45 degree mitre cuts. Mitre one end of a short piece and set it about 1/8th inch above the flush edge of the jamb and the same distance beyond the vertical jamb. Mark the short cut of the mitre at the other end ... again making sure you have allowed the extra 1/8" past the vertical jamb. It should look like a wide "V" with the thicker edge away from the door and the thin portion just above the door.

Using one small nail in the center, tack it into position leaving the head extended out so the board is free to move for adjustment with the vertical trim board. Check that it is 1/8" above the jamb.

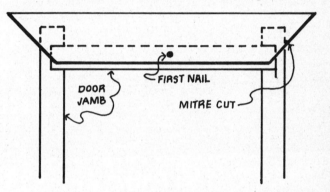

2. The vertical trim board is placed into position with one end on the floor and the other overlapping the mitred cut of the top piece. Mark off on the vertical trim the angle cut that will match the angle of the top board. Make the cut 1/4" oversize to provide margin for any adjustment needed at the mitres. This will be trimmed when squaring off the bottom.

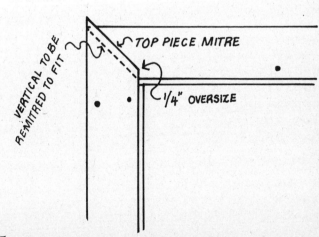

3. Tack the vertical board into position with a single nail and match corners with the top board. Hold this position firmly and tack several additional nails into the vertical board ONLY! Then repeat the steps on the opposite side making certain the top is resting securely on the first vertical trim board before marking the angle. A second nail can be added to the top piece to hold it while working on the second side.

4. If top trim board is set properly on the two vertical boards, it can be nailed in place. Where adjustment is required, pull the tacking nails and reset the top and then nail securely.

5. Recess all nails with a nail set and fill the holes with plastic wood or putty. Sand when dry and apply a sealing coat of shellac, stain or primer--depending on the finish selected. Exactly the same steps are taken to complete the trim on the other entry of the doorway.

6. The door knob is installed to the instructions of the manufacturer. Usually, two screws through the escutcheon plate are required.

As with door trim ... the top piece of window trim is cut and tacked in the center. The sides are next, mitred at the top and square cut at the bottom. Trim is held in place with two rows of #6 recessed finish nails. The outer row is driven into the 2 x 4 framing and the inner row is driven into the window frame.

CEILING TILE

Use, function, room decor and price usually determine the tile selection for any room area. Use can mean several things ... desire for acoustical qualities to add "quiet" to a favorite room; or, serviceability including those qualities which make the surface scrubbable - certainly a consideration for the kitchen area. Others offer an insulating quality of particular value to rooms directly under the roof.

Tiles are usually 12 x 12 inches ... some are made 12 x 24 inches. However, ceiling dimensions seldom result in measurements that will accommodate all "full-size" tiles. A finished ceiling will be more professional looking if border tiles are the same width on opposite walls. A few preliminary steps and a simple formula will enable any homeowner to arrive at correct widths for both the long and short walls.

To find the proper width for border tiles, follow these steps:

1. Measure one of the short walls in the room. If this measurement is not an exact number of feet, take the number of inches left over and add 12. Example: If the short wall measures 12'8", add 12" to the 8" left over. Using the total in the example, divide 20" by 2 ... this will give the width of the border tile for that wall. The border tiles will be 10" wide on each side of the short wall.

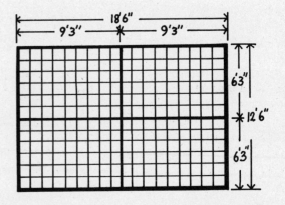

2. Measure one of the long walls in the room. Repeat the procedure to determine width of the border tiles. Example: The wall measures 18'6" ... add 12" to the 6" left over (18") and divide by 2. Border tiles will be 9" at each end.

Open boxes of tiles at least 24 hours before applying to allow adjustment to room temperature and moisture conditions.

Have tools ready to work: automatic stapler filled with 9/16" staples--or hammer and 3d (1 1/8") blued lath nails; cross-cut hand saw or sabre saw; straight-edge; measuring tape; chalk line; 24" or longer carpenter's level; pencil or chalk. For cement application use a good quality ceiling tile adhesive.

Don't apply tile to fresh plaster or green or wet lumber. For furring strips use only a seasoned soft wood like yellow pine. The building should be reasonably dried out before you start your ceilings.

Handle the tiles carefully to avoid damage. Make use of damaged tile at borders and other areas where cutting is necessary to fit tile around light fixtures or other obstructions.

Keep your hands and tools clean to avoid soiling the tile surfaces. Talcum powder in your apron pockets will keep nails clean and hands dry.

3. Corner tiles must be cut to take into account the predetermined widths of both the long and short wall border tiles. Using the same example, the corner tiles would be trimmed to measure 9" x 10". When stapling these corner tiles into position, be certain the proper measurement is located along the respective wall. Mark length on back side of tile edges to avoid mistakes.

4. When cutting border tiles, do not employ short cut method of cutting several at one time ... do each one individually. If wall sheathing is to be installed after the furring strips and tile, edges need not be cut to perfection. The wall sheathing should conceal minor deviations.

Nail with flanges facing out from the wall so both are available for stapling. DO NOT handle tiles without first washing your hands. Smudges on the tile surface can be

difficult to remove. A clean pair of work gloves can be used to help protect the tile surface; smears can sometimes be corrected by dusting with cornstarch.

5. Use 9/16" staples to fasten tiles ... three to each flange. Face-nail the wall edges of border tiles. Slide the tiles firmly into position but take care not to force the corners. Check ridge alignment and staple.

INSTALLING FURRING STRIPS FOR 12 x 12 TILES

Seasoned, dry 1 x 2 or 1 x 3 inch furring strips are recommended framing. Soft pine is best ... pick out straight pieces.

1. The first furring board is nailed across the joist run at right angles flush to the wall.

2. The second strip is nailed so its center is the number of inches determined for the border tile plus 1/2" for the stapling flange. Using the example for determining the correct width of border tile --if the joists run from short wall to short wall, the second furring strip would be positioned and nailed with the center 9 1/2" from the wall.

The purpose of the furring is to provide a solid stapling or glueing base; therefore, the first two boards must be positioned so the narrower tiles along the border can be fastened to wood. Until the opposite wall is reached, full tiles are mounted to the strips that are nailed for 12" centers. The last two boards are placed at the spacing of the first two.

3. Furring strips must provide a true level surface or the tile will have a wavy appearance. Use a long carpenter's level or fashion a straight-edge board four to six feet in length to check level

in both directions. Drive shims
between the strip and joist to
bring it down or hammer tighter
to the joist if it tends to swoop.

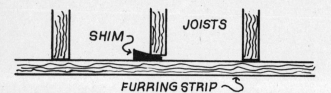

4. In some cases, pipes and electrical wiring hanging below joist
level can be concealed by doubling
up on furring thickness. Install
furring strips parallel to obstruction, then run a second layer
at right angles. Pipes and other
obstructions that still hang below
the ceiling should be framed out
before the tile is installed.

> When applying furring to joists,
> a lot of dust and dirt will be
> dislodged from the floor above.
> Wear goggles to avoid irritation
> or possible damage to the eyes.

5. Check frequently that the lines
formed by the installed tiles are
running true and straight in both
directions.

Tiles are easily cut to fit around
fixtures. Use paper or cardboard
to make a template, transfer shape
to front of tile, cut with a coping saw.

Some 12" x 12" tiles may be installed directly to an existing
ceiling with adhesive if the surface is sound, true and free of
dirt and grease.

Start with small quantity of adhesive, work into the back of
the tile with a putty knife in
the four corners. Apply additional gobs so each spot is about
the size of a golf ball. Keep
adhesive spots about 2 1/2" from
tile edge.

Set the tile lightly against the
existing ceiling about 2" from
previous tile and slip up to
position with increasing pressure as it moves. If surface of
existing ceiling is uneven, increase thickness of the adhesive
load to make surface level with
other tiles. Add more adhesive
where unevenness is particularly
noticeable.

ELEMENTS OF A SUSPENDED CEILING

A suspended grid ceiling consists
of three main elements:

1. Main runners (usually in 12'
lengths)

2. Wall angle (usually in 10' or
12' lengths)

3. Cross tees (usually in 2' and
4' lengths)

The first step is to determine the
finished ceiling height and snap
a chalk line at this level on all
four walls. Use a carpenter's
level around the room. Remember,
final wall sheathing is installed
before the ceiling.

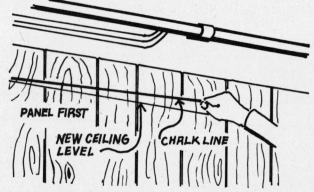

When using standard 24"x 48" ceiling panels, there is a formula
for determining the width of the
border panels so the main runners
and cross tees can be placed in
proper relation to wall edges.

In most cases, main runners are installed perpendicular to the joists and parallel to the long wall. To find the distance the outer runners should be hung from the long wall to achieve same size borders.

1. Measure the length of a short wall and convert into inches. Divide this figure by 48" and, disregarding the full feet, add 48" to the inches left over and divide the total by 2.

EXAMPLE: Assume the short wall is 12'4". Converted to inches (148) divide by 48 and to the odd inches (4) add 48. The total (52) is divided by 2 (26"). This is the width of the border panel and the distance the two outside runners will be located from the long wall

2. To determine the placement of the two outer tees of the other opposite walls, the formula is the same BUT the key number is 24 rather than 48: Measure the long wall and convert to inches. Divide this figure by 24" and, disregarding the full feet, add 24" to the inches left over and divide by 2.

EXAMPLE: Assume the long wall measures 18'6". Converted to inches (222), divide by 24" and add 24 to the odd inches (6). Divide the result (30) by 2 (15). This is the width of the short wall border panels and the distance the outside cross tees will be located from the short wall.

Use a strong platform to stand on when working overhead. This can be built so the added height gives a comfortable working position.

Wall angle is fairly standard among manufacturers but the cross tees and main runners vary in how they inter-connect. Instructions for layout of the grid and installation is generally supplied with the material.

SAWHORSES

A practical and useful device for the homeowner is the sawhorse. Brackets are available which hold the 2 x 4 legs and cross rail.

Pre-drilled holes permit nailing the pieces in place. For a permanent frame, enlarge the holes to accept wood screws.

A handy variation of the standard setup is illustrated. The legs are cut to length so the bottom of the cross rail matches the top of a short ladder.

The platform can be any reasonable length ... 3/4" plywood is cut 12" wide and up to 60" long. Wood screws are spaced along the edge and secured to the rails. A 2 x 4 block on the underside adds support. The ladder steps make it easy to get up and down.

Note that one cross rail is slightly longer than the other. This "overhang" allows fastening of a single bracket upside down. A 2 x 4 in the inverted leg frame becomes a riser for the platform ... which keeps tools and working materials close at hand.

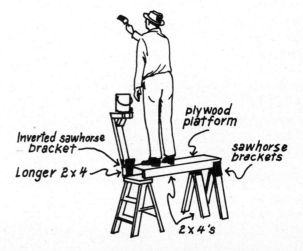

Inverted sawhorse bracket

plywood platform

Longer 2x4

sawhorse brackets

2 x 4's

Laying floor tile

1. Sweep the floor area clean. Concrete must be smooth, dry, clean and free from grease, wax and paint. Smooth off rough spots; fill cracks or holes with a good concrete patching compound. Oil base paint is most easily removed with a floor sanding machine. DON'T USE A FLAMMABLE PAINT REMOVER.

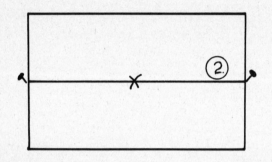

2. Locate the center of the room. Tap nails into the center points of two opposite walls at the base. Disregard offsets and other wall breaks when measuring. Snap a chalkline on the floor.

3. Measure and mark the center of the chalk line. Place a carpenter's square or piece of tile on either side of the line and mark at several points a line perpendicular to the chalk line. Now snap a second chalk line across the first, dividing the room into quarters.

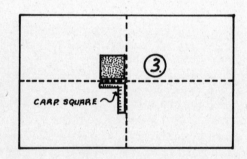

CARP. SQUARE

4. Lay a row of tile along both chalk lines in one of the quarter sections. Overlap the last tile if it is less than a full tile at the wall. If the overlap is less than half a tile along either chalk line, move the entire row past the line 6". This will insure even borders around the room.

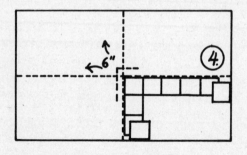

6"

5. Before spreading adhesive, it is important the proper adhesive is used with the type of tile selected. Read and follow the detailed manufacturer's instructions for the specific adhesive to be used and the type of spreader recommended. Work one quandrant at a time.

Spread only the quantity recommended in the directions for your specific adhesive. Spread adhesive to the chalk line, but not on it. If tile has an adhesive backing, merely peel the protective cover off and install.

6. When starting to lay tile, place the first tile exactly at the angle formed by the chalk lines. Set each succeeding tile firmly against the tile already in position and lower it to the adhesive. Keep tiles on guide lines and have corners meet exactly. Do not slide tile into position ... this will cause adhesive to squeeze up between the tiles.

With asphalt or vinyl asbestos tile, work out from center lines. Kneel on the tile, pyramiding out with each succeeding row.

1. Do not roll asbestos or asphalt tile.

2. Do not kneel on freshly laid solid vinyl, crystalline vinyl or cork tile. Use a piece of Masonite or plywood to kneel on.

WORK OUT FROM CENTER

CUTTING TILE

1. Score asphalt tile with a sharp knife; snap off one end of the tile over an edge of lumber or tabletop. Smooth rough edges with sandpaper. For irregular cuts, tile should be heated in an oven or with a blowtorch until pliable, then cut with sturdy scissors. Other types of tile are cut with a sharp knife or scissors. Heating is not required.

2. To cut border tile, place a loose tile directly over the last installed full tile nearest the wall, with the grain running in the same direction, and place another tile flush against the wall on top of the loose tile. A strip of wood in the adhesive will keep the tile clean. Using the

3 TILES - BOTTOM INSTALLED, TOP PLACED OVER, THIRD FROM WALL TO MEASURE CUT ON #2.

top tile as a guide, mark the
first loose tile with a pencil
or sharp awl. Cut and fit into
place.

3. To tile around door jambs, use
a contour gauge or dividers to
draw an outline of the door jamb
on the loose tile to be cut, or
make a paper or cardboard pattern
of the exact shape of the door
jamb frame and transfer this to
the tile. Another way is to saw
about 1/8" from the bottom of
the door jamb and slide the border tile underneath.

4. To fit tile around pipes, cut
a hole where the pipe will go,
then cut the tile from the hole
to the edge.

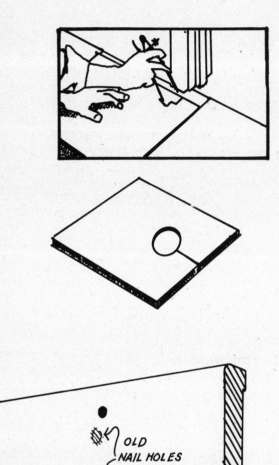

FINISH FLOOR TRIM

When replacing original wood
moldings, do not renail using
the old nail holes. Counter-
sink the heads and fill both
the holes and recesses with a
wood dough. When new wood is
installed, mitre cut the joints
to avoid gaps later on as the
wood shrinks.

A vinyl wall base requires the
wall be free of oil, dirt, any
loose paint ... and the wall
should run right to the floor
or very nearly so.

Apply the adhesive according to
directions; leave approximately
¼" of bare space along the top
and bottom edges so the adhesive will not squeeze out above
the lip.

Immediately press the base firmly against the wall and tight to
the floor. Roll the entire surface with a roller. Exert even
pressure at all points. Press
the toe of the wall base vinyl
tightly against the wall with
a straight edge or length of 2x4.

OLD
NAIL HOLES

BASE SHOE AND MOP BOARD

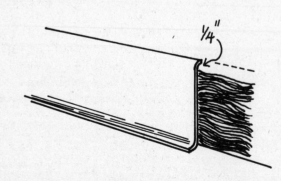

¼"

Typical moulding patterns

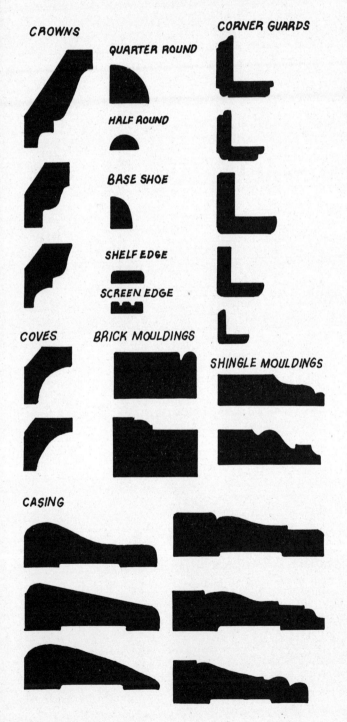

CROWNS

QUARTER ROUND

HALF ROUND

BASE SHOE

SHELF EDGE

SCREEN EDGE

COVES

BRICK MOULDINGS

CASING

CORNER GUARDS

SHINGLE MOULDINGS

Trimming out a recreation room or any room area is relatively easy with the many manufactured trim moldings available today. This section deals with the materials and styling of trim woods and the way to cut, fit and nail the trim to achieve a professional look. Pre-hung windows and doors come with trim already cut to size. This is detailed under "Setting A Pre-hung Door or Window."

These tools are needed:

1. Mitre box (wood or metal)

2. Trim saw (flat blade with fine cross-cut teeth)

3. Light hammer

4. Measuring tape or carpenter's ruler

5. Pencil with a good point

6. Finishing nails (#4, #6 and #8)

7. Square with adjustment for both 90 and 45 degree angles will be helpful when working with long pieces of trim wood.

The profile of various molding styles, casings and baseboards are worth studying. Select a facing style that matches other room trim or sets the desired effect of the room. Two facings of door trim frequently used are illustrated. A more rugged appearance can be achieved by using rough sawn cedar or pine with stain finish.

Outside corner panel joints can be finished with outside corner molding. A cove molding is used for inside corners. If the wall is concrete with furred strips or

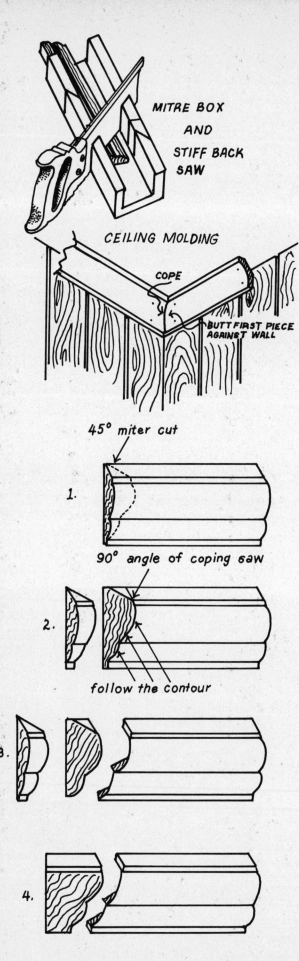

MITRE BOX
AND
STIFF BACK
SAW

CEILING MOLDING

COPE

BUTT FIRST PIECE
AGAINST WALL

45° miter cut

1.

90° angle of coping saw

2.

follow the contour

3.

4.

boxed beams, sanded or rough sawn 1" lumber at the ceiling and floor can add an attractive finished appearance.

Installing trim molding around windows differs slightly from that of doors in that both the top and bottom boards are cut and set in place first. The vertical pieces are marked and cut 1/8" oversize to permit adjustment. The 1/8" setback from the window frame allows for additional movement if necessary. Gaps are filled in with wood putty.

Ceiling, baseboard and corner moldings should be installed in long sections to reduce the number of overlapping mitres where ends are joined. Fewer overlaps also means any wood shrinkage at mitred joints will be less noticeable.

Coping joint is used to form inside corner joints with trim molding.

1. Saw off the end of one abutting member ... square ... as you would for an ordinary butt joint between flat wood members.

2. Butt the square end against the face of the other.

3. Trace the outline of the molding face pattern on the face of the piece beneath the butt end.

4. Mitre the board end that has been traced 45 degrees as indicated.

5. Set the coping saw at a 90 degree angle to the length-wise axis of the mitred end and saw off that portion shown in #3. Follow exactly the face line left by the 45 degree mitred cut.

6. The scrolled end of the molding trim will now match the face of the first member.

Practice makes perfect ... work on scrap pieces before trying the real thing. The money you save is yours.

All rounded molding should be mitre-cut. Straight 1 x 1's can be squared at ends and "butt joined" but mitre cuts improve the over-all appearance of the trim work.

Where a mid-wall joint falls, mitre cut both pieces before installing. The best fit will be obtained by cutting the two ends together. With cove moldings, nail alternately into the wall and ceiling. Outside corners are mitre-cut, inside corners are usually coped.

The base shoe can be purchased ready to cut and install; or, 1" x rough wood or modern door trim molding with the thick side to the floor can be used. Base shoe is similar to quarter-round molding except that it measures 1/2" on the bottom and 3/4" high. It is nailed with the 1/2" side to the floor.

It may prove helpful to paint a first and even a second coat of paint or stain on trim boards before installing. Touch-up painting is easier and faster than the close tolerance brush work required to avoid the adjacent ceiling or wall finish.

¼ ROUND

mitre-cut all rounded molding.

BASESHOE

mitre cut midwall joints.

BASEBOARD

Saw horses make it easier to pre-paint trim.

Use saw horse brackets

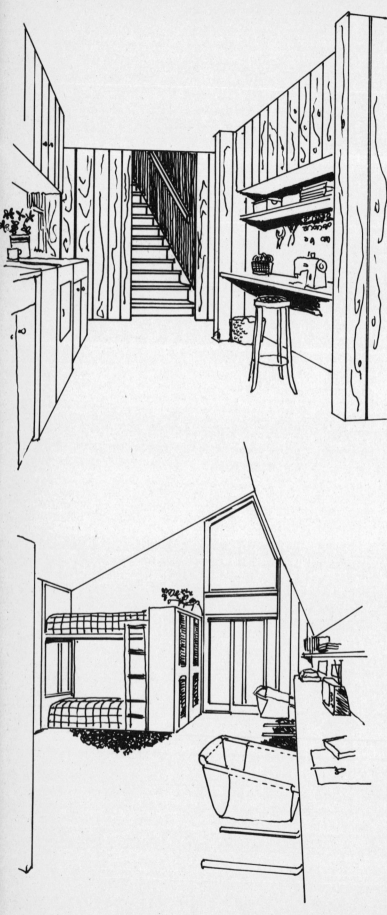

Everything to this point has dealt with basic know-how ... measuring, cutting and fastening materials together, covering up mistakes, planning ahead so costly and time consuming re-do's are avoided. The balance of the book will now make sense. You will see how to apply your new knowledge to specific home improvements and worthwhile maintenance projects.

Improvements which expand living area to your house generally mean added value and a higher sale price when it is time to move. The direct dollar savings can be very substantial when you elect to do all or some of the work yourself.

What you undertake will depend upon your available time and personal interest in completing an improvement like a recreation room or a garage or attic conversion to a family room or extra bedrooms. You may decide to use a professional for some or all of the work. Can you still save money? Yes!

Review the material in this book to learn everything you can about the improvement you have in mind. Look through magazines for interesting designs and decor ideas. Visit suppliers to look over standard as well as new materials now available. Check prices so you have a basis for evaluating contractor bids.

Now prepare a list of specific materials, hardware and finishes you want used. Include any special construction details ... things out of the norm such as curved wall, brick fireplace, etc. ... to be completed by the contractor. If you plan to do some of the work yourself, state exactly where the contractor's work will stop and you will take over. However, contractors are very reluctant to have a homeowner schedule do-it-yourself work in the middle of his work schedule.

Pick several reputable contractors in the area you would like to have submit bids. Who is reputable? You might contact your better business bureau to learn if customer complaints have been registered against any of the ones you have selected to contact. Most reliable builders and remodelers will have been in business for some time.

Each of the contractors should be given a copy of the specifications so that bids will be based on common ground rules. At the same time, ask for the names and addresses or phone numbers of other homeowners they have done similar work for. When following up on these contacts, be sure to ask enough detailed questions for a good evaluation.

Sticking doors & windows

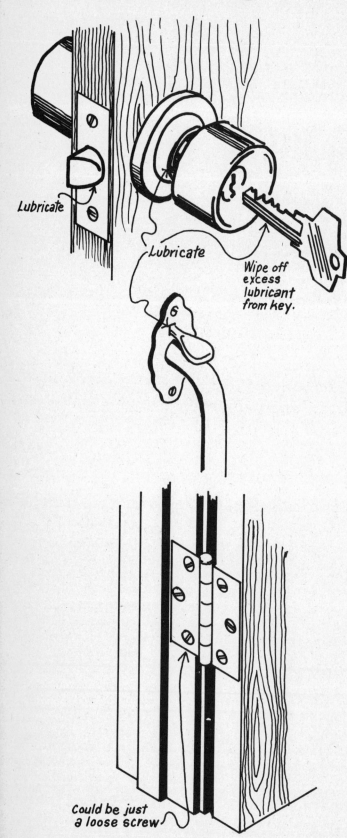

Lubricate

Lubricate

Wipe off excess lubricant from key.

Could be just a loose screw.

Sticky locks, doors and windows are common irritations that are easily corrected with just a little know-how and patience. Door mechanisms can get gummed up over a period of time as dust congeals with the old lubricating oil or grease used in years past. You know the problem is starting when door knobs and latches begin to respond slowly ... eventually they will stick. New lubricants with a silicone base offer a quick way to spray away dirt and old grease around the door knob shaft and latch. One such product, WD-40 and others similar to it, stops squeaks, removes rust, even displaces moisture while leaving a fine coat of lubricant; only drips should be wiped off ... the carrier evaporates leaving the film coating.

These lubricants can also be used on aluminum without leaving a black oily residue. Sticking storm windows and doors can be eased quickly. <u>Note</u>: It is not advisable to spray directly into a key lock because certain types of tumblers operate on friction to turn the latch or lock. Instead, spray the key, insert it in the lock and turn it several times. Repeat if necessary.

Doors are something else ... corrective action may be as simple as tightening a screw or as time consuming as planing down a hinged edge.

Exterior doors are usually solid wood with or without decorative facings and window ports. A front entrance single door is generally 36" wide while rear entrance doors are more often 32". Unless special ordered, doors are 6'8" high. Exterior doors generally employ three hinges while interior doors use two. Hinges are recessed in

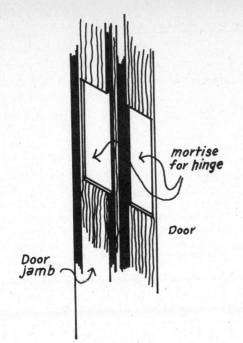

mortise
for hinge

Door

Door
jamb

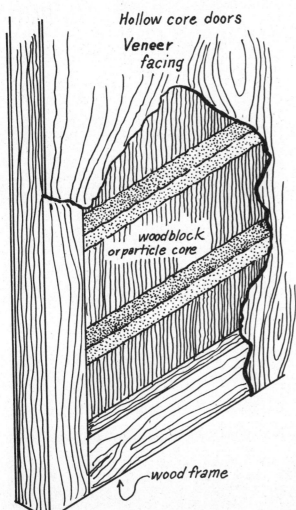

Hollow core doors

Veneer
facing

woodblock
or particle core

wood frame

TYPICAL WOOD VENEERS ARE:
LUAN • MAHOGONY • BIRCH • ASH

both the door edge and jamb so the hinge surface, when installed, is flush with the wood surface. The cutout area is referred to as "mortise."

The high cost of a solid door today has brought the hollow core door into exterior use as well as its common application for interior use. "Hollow core" refers to a door that is manufactured with framing ... the pieces being approximately 3" deep at bottom and top plus connecting side rails about 1 1/4" wide. An extra block is added to the side rail where the knob and latch mechanism is installed. The sheathing is usually a wood facing about 3/16" thick, made of a base wood laminated to a natural wood veneer roughly 1/64" thick.

Well-constructed hollow core door resists warp and twist but is somewhat subject to puncture-type damage. Hollow core doors can be shortened up to 1" on the top and bottom but NOT a total 2" from either end. Most door length adjustments are made at the bottom edge in order to gain clearance over carpeting.

Inside doors in older houses may be of a solid wood construction. The value of this type of door has increased enormously in recent years so refinishing may be both a practical and profitable project for the homeowner. Depending upon the surface condition, the doors can be stripped to bare wood, then varnished for the natural look, stained and then varnished for specific tones, antiqued or simply painted. Where remodeling plans require the replacement of solid doors with hollow core, don't chuck them or give them away ... check with interior decorators or those companies supplying "old" doors to contractors. Good ones could be worth considerable money to you.

71

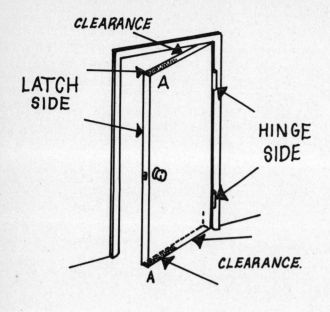

CLEARANCE

LATCH SIDE

HINGE SIDE

A

CLEARANCE.

A

When doors stick or fail to shut, the causes might be as basic as loose hinge screws, a bent hinge or a door frame that has worked itself out of square. Humidity sometimes causes a temporary binding, but this condition corrects itself as moisture levels decrease.

Just where the door is binding will determine the corrective measures to take. Study the illustrations ... note the arrows pointing to common problem spots ... then follow these corrective steps:

1. DOOR BINDS ON THE LATCH SIDE. This normally occurs at the top corner or the corresponding spot on the bottom edge (shaded areas "A"). First check for bent hinge or loose hinge screws just needing tightening. If one or more do not turn down firmly, try a longer screw that will penetrate to solid wood beneath the hinge. An alternative to the longer screw is to fill in the screw holes with wood fill, wood plugs or small doweling. The wood pieces are dipped in glue and then tapped into the hole with a hammer ... gently! When dry, the excess is cut off flush. With the hinge held in place, mark and drill a pilot hole for each screw and reinstall the hinge. In the case of a bent hinge or pin, replace it.

If the problem has not been corrected, the next step is to add cardboard shims behind the door or jamb hinge. In other words, a door binding at the top "A" would require cardboard shims behind the upper hinge to force the top corner forward and down. More than one thickness of cardboard may be required. To save time by not having to completely remove each screw, notches can be cut in cardboard shims as illustrated. They can be slipped into posi-

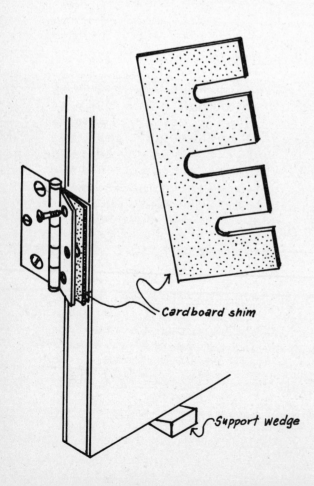

Cardboard shim

Support wedge

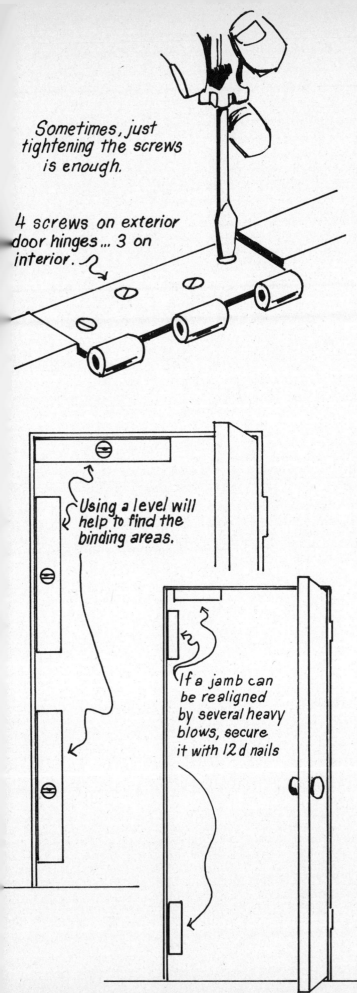

Sometimes, just tightening the screws is enough.

4 screws on exterior door hinges ... 3 on interior.

Using a level will help to find the binding areas.

If a jamb can be realigned by several heavy blows, secure it with 12d nails

tion beneath the hinge and the screws merely tightened. Check the open-and-close action carefully before adding additional shims ... too much buildup might shift the bind to another point.

2. DOOR BINDS ALONG THE HINGE SIDE. This is normally caused when the mortised area is too deep and the hinge face is below the wood surface. The net affect is the door edge closes against the wood jamb and this can place undue strain on the hinge. The problem is corrected by shimming all hinges sufficiently to bring the surfaces flush with the jamb and/or door edge.

3. DOOR FRAMING OUT OF SQUARE. Jambs can shift as a house settles, the framing lumber dries out and road traffic and other vibrations over a period of years work fastening nails loose. Merely driving the same nails in again won't solve the problem for long. New nails should be added. The tools required are a hammer and a 2x4 or other suitable protecting block of wood plus some 12d nails.

With the door in a fully opened position, place the block near the top of the jamb on the hinge side and strike the block several heavy blows with the hammer. Test the door swing. If the bind has been eased, drive three 12d finishing nails into the jamb in the area that was hammered. This will hold it in position. Countersink each nail head and fill the holes with a wood filler or Spackle. Touch up to match the existing finish. In some cases, the block and hammer treatment may have to be applied to the bottom of the hinge side jamb and across the top as well. Don't overdo it ... test frequently. When the binding has eased, STOP! When nailing and countersinking, exercise care that the hammer head does not hit and damage the jamb surface.

4. SANDING, PLANING OR POWER CUTTING. If none of the foregoing "cures" solve the problem or the binding occurs along an entire edge of the door, the excess will have to be sanded or planed. Sanding works well when high spots on the door edge are the cause of the bind. Use a medium or fine grit sandpaper with a wood sanding block. Move the block back and forth along the edge with the grain, <u>not</u> across it. An orbital, straight or dual-action power sander can also be used. A sanding disc attachment on a power drill is NOT recommended because it can cut much too fast even with a fine grit paper, plus the inherent difficulty of retaining a flat edge free of scallops, waves or scars.

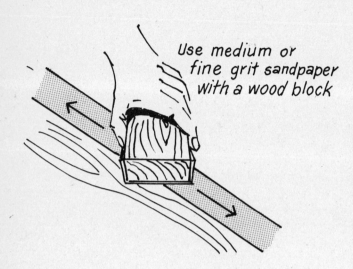

Use medium or fine grit sandpaper with a wood block

A hand plane can be used when a full edge length has to be reduced, as might be required when a replacement door has to be modified to fit an existing jamb. In certain instances it might be practical to use a power sabre saw or circular saw with a straight-edge guide when a quarter inch or more has to be removed. Measure carefully and cut to the outside of the mark line ... you can always take a little more off with a plane or sander. When working on hollow core doors, use masking tape on both sides at the cut line to prevent splintering of the wood face. The veneer will splinter in much the same way as paneling or plywood. A light sanding should follow, and the bottom edges can be rounded slightly to reduce wear and tear on carpeting.

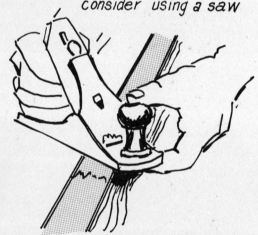

A hand plane can be used for reducing full edge length up to 1/4 inch. Over 1/4 inch — consider using a saw

When a hinged side of a door has been sanded, planed or saw cut, it will be necessary to remove the hinges and re-mortise the hinge recess so each is flush with the wood surface when re-installed. A chisel should be adequate for cutting out the added depth. Go slow ... test frequently as the depth is increased by inserting the hinge and rubbing a finger across the joint.

You may need to remortise the hinge recess. Use a chisel.

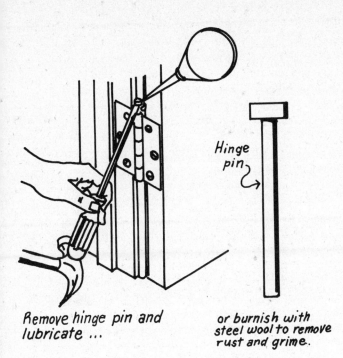

Remove hinge pin and lubricate ...

or burnish with steel wool to remove rust and grime.

Cardboard shim will raise latch catch.

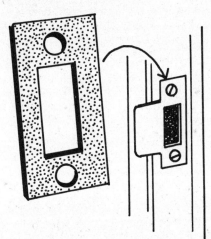

Resetting door stop will end a rattle.

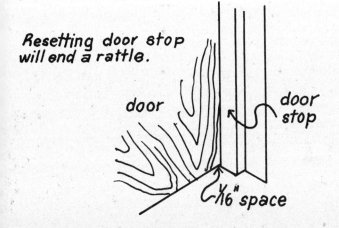

door

door stop

1/16" space

All sanded, planed or cut surfaces should be refinished with appropriate sealer and final coat.

5. OTHER DOOR PROBLEMS. Squeaking door hinges are either rusty or the lubricant has worn away. Remove the hinge pins one at a time and burnish with steel wool or scouring pad to remove rust and grime. Spray the hinge and pin with a silicone lubricant and re-install. Use a cardboard or similar shield to protect adjacent wall surfaces, carpeting, etc. Repeat with each hinge.

Occasionally a door will shrink to a point where the latch no longer catches behind the striker plate. Shims can be added behind the latch striker plate and also behind the door hinges. The best results are gained when hinge shims are added first. If a couple of cardboard shims behind the hinges fail to bring the latch catch behind the plate, then remove the screws from the striker plate, fashion cardboard shims to match the opening and screw positions of the plate and re-install.

CAUTION: A striker plate offset from the wood surface can catch and snag or tear clothing; therefore, round the edges with a file to avoid the problem.

To correct a door that rattles when closed, remove the door stop and re-install approximately 1/16" from the door when it is in a closed position. Use finishing brads to secure to the jamb, recess the heads and add wood fill.

Touch up as required to match original finish.

STICKING WINDOWS

High moisture conditions may cause windows to stick temporarily but more often than not the problem is created by paint. When precautions are not taken, paint can

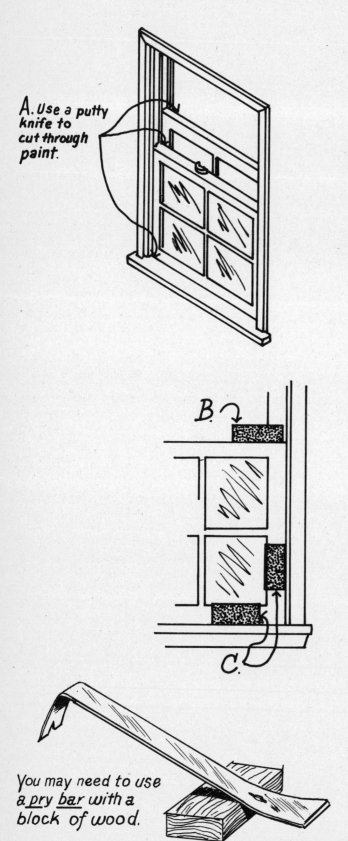

A. Use a putty knife to cut through paint.

You may need to use a pry bar with a block of wood.

run between the window frame and guide tracks or the window facing and sill. Left for a period of time, the paint drips harden and resist any movement whatsoever.

Where a window has been stuck closed for some time:

1. Look for paint or varnish ("A") on both the sides and the facing portions of the sill as well as the crack between the top and bottom window sections. Use a single edge razor blade, a thin sharp knife or putty knife to cut through to the frame. Sometimes oil base paint in the track can be softened sufficiently by dripping turpentine from an eye dropper down the track. Wait a few minutes before attempting to break the bind. Then ...

2. Using a block of wood and a hammer, place the block on the top edge of the window ("B") and strike several sharp blows "downward" as if trying to shut the bottom window section. This technique sometimes breaks the paint seal better than an upward force and is less apt to damage the window. A block and hammer can also be used along the side edges and bottom of the window ("C") but the sharpness of the blow must be considerably less to protect the glass. The window may not free up the first time, so repeat each step ... the blade around the window cracks, the turpentine down the track and the sharp blow from both corners at the top of the window.

3. If the window still does not open, it may be necessary to "force" pry from the outside. The flat edge of a crowbar will generally do the trick. Use a block under the crowbar for both added leverage and to prevent scaring of the outside sill surface.

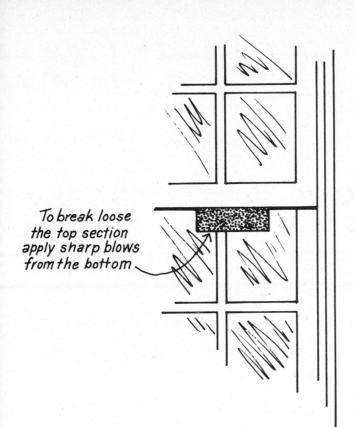

To break loose the top section apply sharp blows from the bottom

4. Top window sections are more difficult to free because turpentine cannot be dripped "upwards" and the window frame itself is not as strong as the lower section. When using the hammer and block, sharp blows to the closed position will have to be applied from underneath. In severe cases it may be necessary to remove the entire window casing ... a job only for a carpenter or very experienced do-it-yourselfer.

5. When a paint-bound window is freed up or a working window is simply difficult to open and shut a silicone or graphite-type lubricant, soap or paraffin can be applied to all friction point. In the case of metal sashes and tracks, remove any paint or rust with steel wool and then apply one of the lubricants listed above. Wood sashes and guides can be treated in the same manner except a fine grit sandpaper should be used to remove paint.

SECURITY

Auxiliary locks for both doors and windows can provide a secondary level of protection against forced entry. When selecting an auxiliary lock, the key word is QUALITY! Cheap locks can be opened easily and quickly by any professional thief; furthermore, working parts tend to wear out more quickly and it becomes very frustrating as the lock becomes more difficult to operate.

JIMMY-PROOF LOCKS use an interlocking bolt mechanism of cylinder construction. With this type of lock, entry is impossible without a key so the only alternative is to break the door.

DEAD LOCKS offer a high level of security. However, the lock bolt is turned by hand rather than a key so it is not suitable for doors with glass or screen which could be broken to gain entry.

NIGHT LATCHES utilize an automatic locking feature. The lock bolt face is constructed on a 45 degree angle. This angle lets it retract as the bolt hits the keeper, then snap in behind the keeper as soon as it clears.

A VENTILATING LOCK is a stop-position type which permits opening of the window slightly for ventilation, yet preventing further action.

Since a key is needed, this is an excellent lock for windows and doors with glass.

There are two auxiliary window locks ... the SASH LOCK uses a key, is installed with "one-way" screws to discourage removal. With the key lock, even a broken window will not allow the sash to be raised.

Shelving

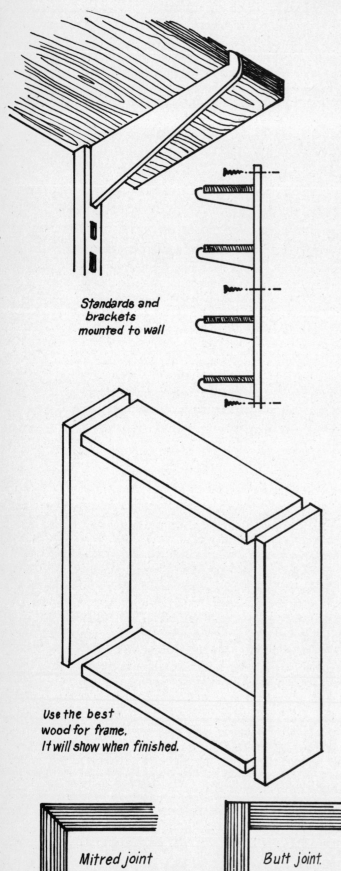

Standards and brackets mounted to wall

Use the best wood for frame. It will show when finished.

Mitred joint

Butt joint.

Shelving for books, bric-a-brac, stereo speakers, etc. can be as simple as attaching wall standards with screws, snapping in the appropriate bracket and laying on shelving. By the same token, it can involve a complete custom-built wall-hung cabinet or free-standing floor unit.

Metal standards with shelf brackets or clips offer adjustable height, are available in different lengths, styles and finishes. Manufacturers produce different shaped slots ... make sure the bracket hooks match the slots. The other important thing when adding shelving of this type is to make sure the shelf wood to be used has been kiln dried and has no warp or twist. Many sizes of shelving are now available pre-finished and wrapped in a see-through protective covering.

If you choose to build an enclosed unit with shelves, follow these steps:

1. Determine the number and the height, length and depth of shelves desired. Hand-select 1" clear pine or other appropriate lumber in the width that will produce the needed depth for the shelves. Be sure to let the wood adjust to room temperature and humidity at least several days prior to using.

2. Cut two pieces the same length-- for the top and bottom; then, two more for the side framing. If there is a difference, use the best wood pieces for the top and sides when the ultimate finish will show the grain in either natural or stained tones.

3. The elements can be butt joined or, for the professional look, mitered. They can be fastened together with #6 finishing nails, but a more rigid frame will result from using 1 3/4" thin-shaft wood screws.

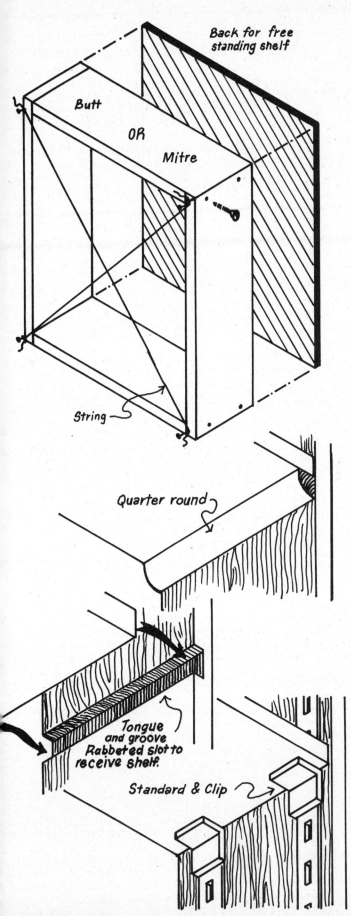

Back for free standing shelf

Butt

OR

Mitre

String

Quarter round

Tongue and groove
Rabbeted slot to receive shelf.

Standard & Clip

Stand the ends upright and use some 2x4 blocks or bricks on either side to hold them in place while setting the top piece into position. With mitered joints, small brads can be used to temporarily hold the joints together while drilling appropriate size holes through the top and side. The depth of the drilled hole should be approximately 3/4's of the screw length. Three screw holes spaced evenly along each joint should be sufficient. The same procedures are repeated for each joint.

4. Each hole is then countersunk to receive the screw heads. The depth should be just enough so the screw head itself is below the surface and the space can be filled with a wood filler. The screws are turned in about half way. Then, string or wire can be stretched diagonally ... see illustration ... across the opening to help hold the frame square while the screws are being set. A spot of glue along each joint will add strength.

5. The end supports for shelving can be metal standards with clips or wood pieces such as quarter round or base shoe with one of the flat edges facing up. Carefully measure for the correct shelf position on each side; run a string between the two marks and check it with a level. Make any adjustments, then secure the wood supports using glue plus several brads to hold them in position while the glue sets up.

6. If the shelf is to be free standing, a backing of hardboard or thin plywood can be cut to fit ... then nailed, screwed or glued to the back. It is a good idea to keep the diagonal strings in place until this has been completed. The shelf cabinet is now ready for prime coat and finish.

Building a bar

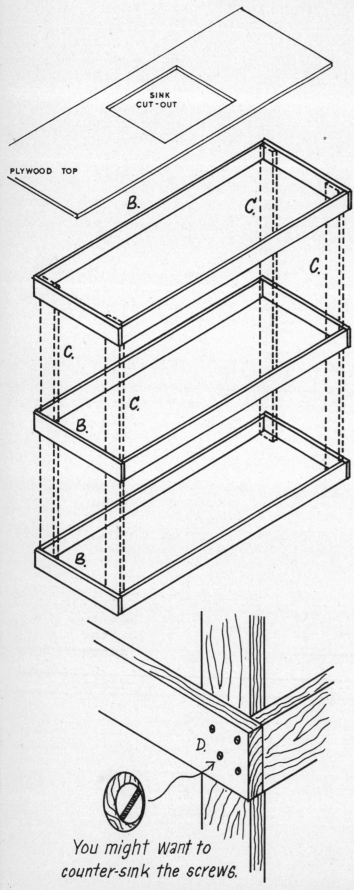

SINK CUT-OUT

PLYWOOD TOP

B.

C.

C.

C.

C.

B.

B.

D.

You might want to counter-sink the screws.

The space available and the desired prominence of the bar will determine the size and final finish. While constructing your own bar, refer to the illustrations as you move to each step. You should find it easy to build and fully serviceable.

A. Determine overall length and depth ... the exterior facing you want and how the top is finished: paint, stain, contact-type vinyl, etc. Allow enough depth for a sink and enough overhang for knee-room when seated.

B. Cut six 1 x 4's to the overall length ... six 1 x 4's to the depth. Nail together three box frames as illustrated using 1 1/2" coated box or finish nails. From the drawing, you can see that one box forms the top, one the bottom and the third acts to strengthen the entire frame.

C. Cut four 1 x 4's to height for vertical support of the box frames. Starting at the bottom, nail the uprights into the corners with 2" nails to hold everything in place for Step D. If the bar is more than five feet long, add vertical supports in the middle of the long sides to stiffen the framing.

If a side enclosure is planned, make frame supports as above. Where a sink is to be located along the side rather than in back, a shelf at work height should be added ... large enough to support the sink.

D. Counter-drill and screw together all joints with #10 x 1 1/2" flathead wood screws. While nailing might give adequate support, the wood screws help to stiffen the frame and eliminate wobble.

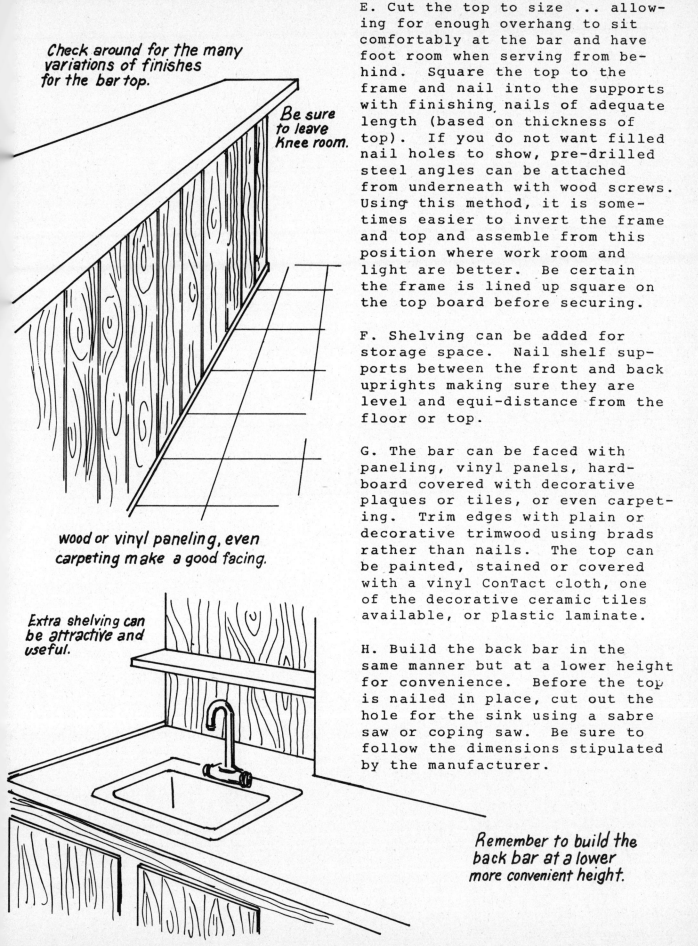

Check around for the many variations of finishes for the bar top.

Be sure to leave knee room.

wood or vinyl paneling, even carpeting make a good facing.

Extra shelving can be attractive and useful.

Remember to build the back bar at a lower more convenient height.

E. Cut the top to size ... allowing for enough overhang to sit comfortably at the bar and have foot room when serving from behind. Square the top to the frame and nail into the supports with finishing nails of adequate length (based on thickness of top). If you do not want filled nail holes to show, pre-drilled steel angles can be attached from underneath with wood screws. Using this method, it is sometimes easier to invert the frame and top and assemble from this position where work room and light are better. Be certain the frame is lined up square on the top board before securing.

F. Shelving can be added for storage space. Nail shelf supports between the front and back uprights making sure they are level and equi-distance from the floor or top.

G. The bar can be faced with paneling, vinyl panels, hardboard covered with decorative plaques or tiles, or even carpeting. Trim edges with plain or decorative trimwood using brads rather than nails. The top can be painted, stained or covered with a vinyl ConTact cloth, one of the decorative ceramic tiles available, or plastic laminate.

H. Build the back bar in the same manner but at a lower height for convenience. Before the top is nailed in place, cut out the hole for the sink using a sabre saw or coping saw. Be sure to follow the dimensions stipulated by the manufacturer.

Improving basement stairway

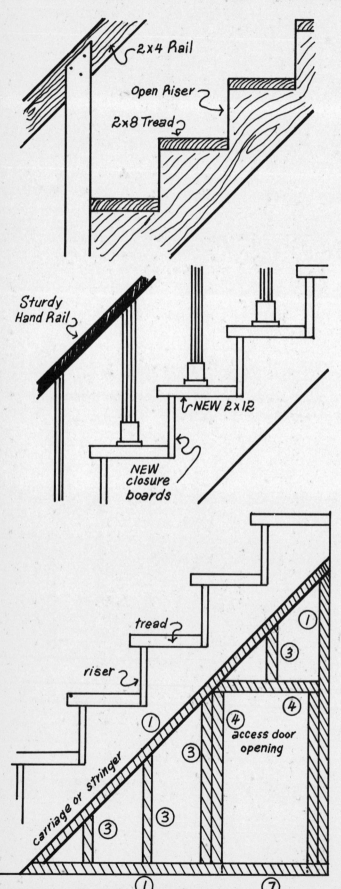

2x4 Rail

Open Riser

2x8 Tread

Sturdy Hand Rail

NEW 2x12

NEW closure boards

tread

riser

carriage or stringer

access door opening

The first illustration depicts a typical stairway to a basement. The handrail is a common 2x4 which is often mounted on one side only. The stair treads are the shallowest permitted by code, 2x8 ... and they are both unsafe and uncomfortable. In most instances, they do not have risers so the toe can slip forward and the result is a barked shin. If you are planning to finish a basement area, safety and comfort can be added to the stairway with a minimum of work or extra cost.

This drawing shows the same stairway improved. The original 2x4 handrail has been replaced with an attractive bannister ... the small treads have been taken out and replaced with 2x10's and the riser portion of the stair has been enclosed with 1x8's. Where very small children are about, a second handrail mounted below the standard rail is a decided safety addition.

Where an open stairway leads to the basement, the space underneath is easily converted to storage area complete with a door. After the basic improvements have been made to the stairway, a simple enclosure can be built:

1. Measure and cut the 2x4 bottom plate, the angled top plate and the longest stud. The joints forming the angle should be mitered. Nail these elements together on the floor.

2. Set the 2x4 frame in place beneath the stringer to check fit. Make necessary adjustments before proceeding.

3. Measure, cut and miter the tops of the remaining 2x4 studs and end nail within the frame on standard 16" centers or 24" centers which

are acceptable for this type of
framing. The rough-in for the
door frame should be completed if
the entry is from the side; otherwise, it is framed in separately
at the open end.

4. Set the complete wall frame in
place. The top (angled) plate
will run under the stringer but
set back the thickness of the
sheathing to be used. In other
words, 1/2" drywall will require
a 1/2" setback to produce a flush
surface.

5. Where the stairway is open on
both sides, a second frame will
be constructed. Door framing for
the end should be put in as described in Carpentry I.

6. Install finish sheathing.

7. Cut out the bottom plate within the doorway and hang the door.

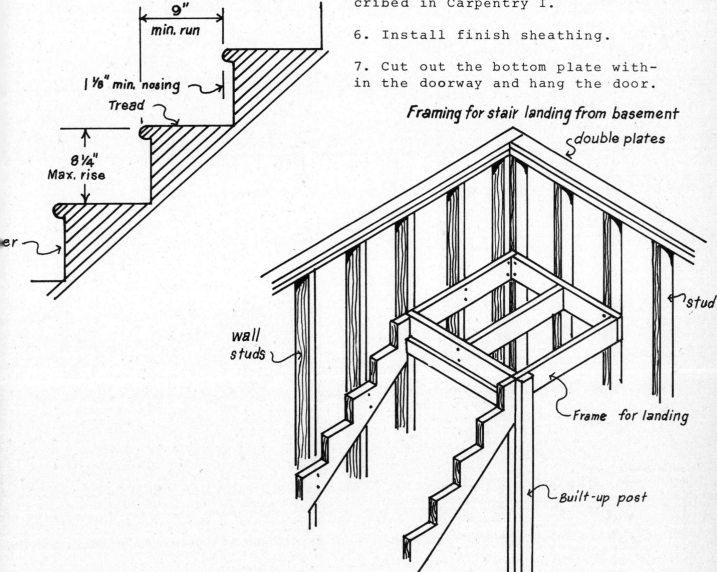

Closed stair dimensions

9"
min. run

1 ⅛" min. nosing

Tread

8 ¼"
Max. rise

er

Framing for stair landing from basement

double plates

wall
studs

stud

Frame for landing

Built-up post

83

Converting a basement area

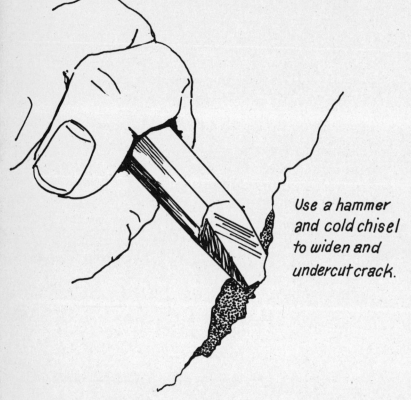

Use a hammer and cold chisel to widen and undercut crack.

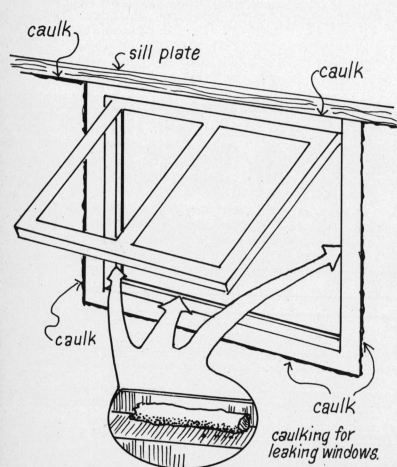

caulk

sill plate

caulk

caulk

caulk

caulking for leaking windows.

PREPARATION OF BASEMENT AREA WALLS

With planning and material ordering completed, the next thing is the actual construction. The ver first step is to check for water leaks and potential water leak areas.

1. Any cracks in the foundation wall or floor, whether indicating leaking or not, should be repaired. Using a cold chisel and hamme widen and undercut the cracks slightly to give patching compoun an "edge" to hold it in place. Wear protective goggles. Fill cracks with a good quality patching compound ... epoxy types generally work best. Follow manufacturer's instructions.

2. The next step is caulking alon the perimeter sill plates and sea. ing casement windows. Use a good top quality Butyl or latex caulk ... they are waterproof and stay flexible for many years. Force caulk well into the space between the plate and foundation and also around the casement window frame.

Casement windows may be leakproofed by opening the window and laying a 1/4" bead of caulk along both mating surfaces. When the window is closed, the caulking forms a seal. Do not use caulk that hardens.

3. If foundation walls are to be painted, the third step is to seal and waterproof the masonry. Several types of plastic and latex-based sealants are available and each has a little different formula. Follow the manufacturer's instructions for preparation and application as they can vary. Sealing is not necessary if studwall framing or furring is planned unless a notice-

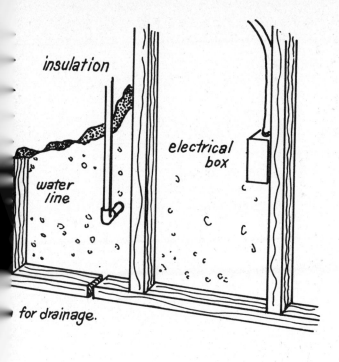

insulation

water line

electrical box

for drainage.

able moisture problem exists. However, some homeowners prefer the extra protection despite the added work.

4. Basement walls are generally framed with standard 2 x 4 studs. This allows enough depth to install 3 1/2" batt insulation. The use of standard size electrical boxes allows for routing waterlines necessary for wet bar, laundry, shop area, etc. Where a drain line is required along a length of wall, build the stud frame with 2 x 6's or set 2 x 4's away from the masonry wall so drain pipe can fit between the masonry and stud walls. Insulate waterlines before closing up the wall.

Remember to notch wall bottom plates beneath windows, the water entrance valve and other potential water leak areas.

5. Perimeter walls can also be constructed with 2 x 2's or furred with 1 x 4's. They are fastened directly to the masonry wall with adhesive and hardened nails. Of course, plumbing lines cannot be routed through them. Also, a shallow-type electrical box must be used, and this is difficult when working with the new code-required 3-wire cable.

6. Before an assembled wall section is raised into position, staple a 4-mil vapor barrier to the side that will face the foundation wall. This polyethelene barrier should extend from the top plate down and under the bottom plate with about 6" extra on the floor when the wall section is raised. This can be cut off later when flooring is installed.

7. When insulating, built-in vapor barrier or batt insulation should face the room area. Insulation should be behind any water lines and electric cables. Remember to insulate along the perimeter sill plate between the joists.

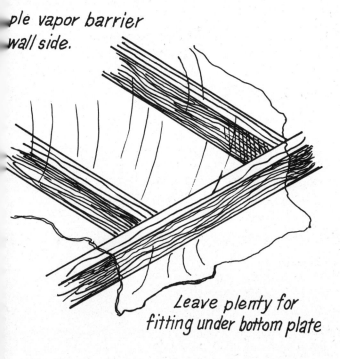

ple vapor barrier wall side.

Leave plenty for fitting under bottom plate

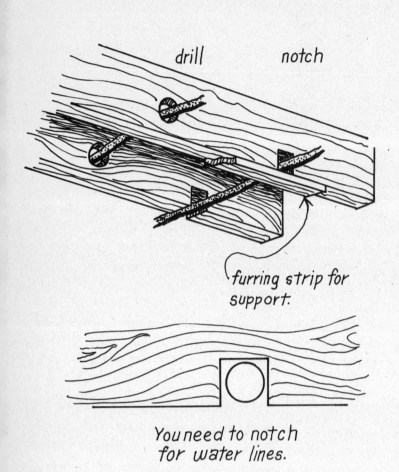

drill   notch

furring strip for support.

You need to notch for water lines.

Frame around I-beam
exist 2x8 plate

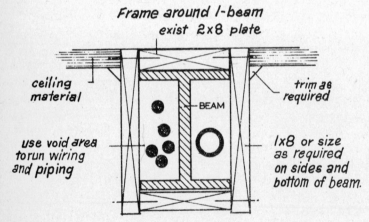

ceiling material

trim as required

BEAM

use void area to run wiring and piping

1x8 or size as required on sides and bottom of beam.

Frame for plumbing stack

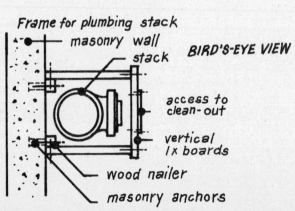

masonry wall
stack

BIRD'S-EYE VIEW

access to clean-out

vertical 1x boards

wood nailer

masonry anchors

RAISING BASEMENT OBSTRUCTIONS

A problem sometimes encountered when finishing a basement is maintaining adequate headroom. Basements often measure 7 feet from joists to floor and even less under "I" beams and heat ducts. Short of raising the whole house off its foundation, there is no practical way to increase existing basement headroom. Therefore, with only minimum clearance available, it might mean raising anything which hangs below the joists

The least difficult to re-arrange is electrical wiring and telephone cable. Two methods can be used. The quickest and easiest being the notching of the underside of joists and securing the wires in the recess. They must be supported with staples or furring strips nailed across the notches. The second method involves drilling holes through each joist large enough to carry the wires. The disadvantage, of course, is having to disconnect one end of each wire in order to thread it through the drilled holes.

Water line pipes can present anothe headroom problem when they are stra hung below joists level or run perpendicular to the joists. Raising them can involve work because few pipe runs offer enough "spring" to permit forcing them into notch-out Therefore, each such pipe run must be disconnected at some point, rerouted with appropriate fittings to change the direction and then recor nect.

Vertical pipes along the face of a foundation wall can be boxed in. Even when plans call for leaving th concrete exposed ... perhaps painte or smooth coated ... rough cedar or other lumber can be used to conceal them attractively.

An even more difficult pipe moving situation involves horizontal drain lines below joist level. Unless ceiling height is in a critical range, box them in. In urban areas

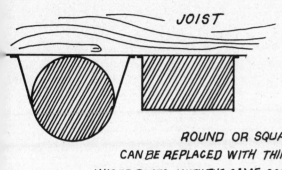

JOIST

ROUND OR SQUARE DUCTS
CAN BE REPLACED WITH THINNER
WIDER DUCTS WITH THE SAME SQUARE INCH
AIR FLOW CAPACITY.

NEW FLAT DUCT

2 inch inset

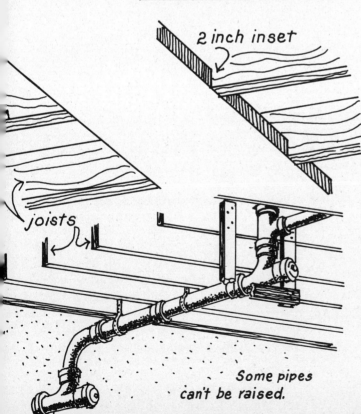

joists

Some pipes
can't be raised.

drain pipe modifications require an experienced plumber because of safety factors. Under certain conditions, a second joist must be nailed to each notched joist to pick up strength lost in notching for large diameter drain pipe. Any cut more than one-fourth into a support, such as a joist, requires that type of strengthening.

Heating ducts can also reduce headroom. The first solution to consider is replacing round or thick square duct with a wide but thin shape, especially where only one or two short modifications are involved. Changing out long duct runs can be expensive plus a great deal of work. But it can be done. However, make sure any replacement duct is designed to carry the same square inch volume of air flow or heating can be affected adversely.

Replace across-joist duct runs with 2" deep by required width to accept the inset of the thin duct and gain a flush ceiling and full headroom. If this is too much work and expense, adapt only the worst offenders within traffic areas and box in the rest. Incidentally, placement of heavy or permanent objects, such as planters and furniture, can "direct" traffic away from areas where low "head-bangers" exist. Plan ahead and whip the problem before it occurs.

INSTALLING BASEMENT FLOORING

Even with cushioned carpeting, a concrete floor is hard and very often cold. A raised floor can ease both conditions but sub-flooring cuts down on headroom. Therefore, the flooring installed must be as thin as practical. The easiest to install is a network of 1 x 4's covered with plywood. This sub-flooring can then be covered with tile or carpeting. The entire space becomes very livable on a year-round basis.

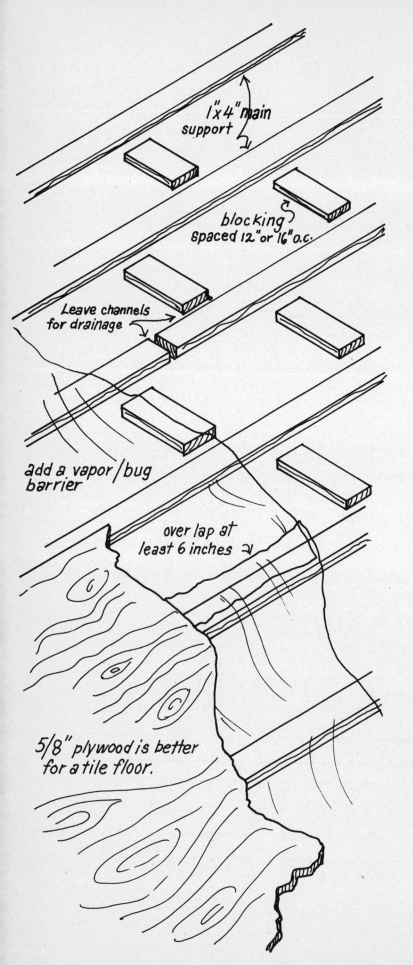

1"x4" main support

blocking spaced 12" or 16" o.c.

Leave channels for drainage

add a vapor/bug barrier

over lap at least 6 inches

5/8" plywood is better for a tile floor.

1. Lay out a supporting network o
1 x 4's on 12" or 16" centers. I
1/2" plywood or its equivalent is
to be the underlayment, use 12"
centers; with 5/8" plywood, 16"
centers are adequate. Order exterior grade plywood. The boards
are layed flat. Short pieces of
1 x 4 are then spaced between the
main runs as blocking.

2. An important precaution is to
cut weep channels in the undersid
of the 1 x 4's before glueing in
place. These channel sawouts
should lead from window wells or
other potential water sources toward the floor drain. In the
event of water or condensation
forming on the walls, the channels allow accumulated water to
flow to the drain.

3. The 1 x 4 grid can be attached
to the floor or not. If attached,
use a waterproof mastic with a
caulking gun. This method is fast,
secure and less work than driving
masonry nails. Do not attach all
of the 1 x 4's. In the event of
flooding, it might be necessary to
get them up. Plan it out by drawing a layout on grid paper. Attach only the 1 x 4's where sheets
of plywood will abut. Suggestion: Install floor after all
walls have been erected. Then,
any section can be removed without disturbing the walls.

4. Staple a vapor/bug barrier over
the 1 x 4's. Start at perimeter
walls and work toward the drain,
overlapping the 4-mil polyethylene
at least 6". Installing in this
manner prevents catching a water
flow between overlaps. Staple
to alternate boards.

5. The last material to be install
ed is the plywood underlayment.
Grade used is dependent upon ultimate floor covering to be used ...
B-C or B-D for tile and C-C or C-D
for carpet. H O W recommends 5/8"
plywood; 1/2" is adequate but it
does allow some "spring," and
floor tiles could work loose.

Finishing an attic

PRELIMINARY CONSIDERATIONS

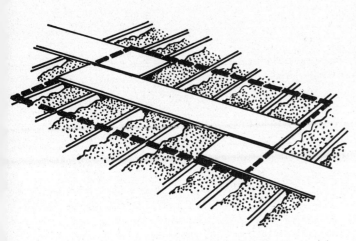

The first consideration is whether a finished attic area will provide enough usable space to make the project worthwhile. The sloping roof can mislead the untrained eye as to how much usable area is actually available. Don't just estimate by eye, measure it! If some type of walking surface (partial or complete flooring) is not already there, lay down something like plywood or 1" planking to walk on. A 5/8" or 3/4" sheet of 4 x 8' plywood cut into three strips 16" x 8' produces 24' of walking surface which can be used later as permanent flooring.

Minimum ceiling clearance for comfortable headroom is 7'. Installed flooring and ceiling materials take up 2" to 5" (1" to 1 1/2" for flooring, 1" to 4" for ceiling). Therefore, a minimum height of 7'2" to 7'5" must be allowed for a 7' finished ceiling height. Using a plumbline and measuring tape, determine the maximum width of full height walking area in the attic. Run a vertical string from joist to the point on rafters on both sides of the ridgebeam to help visualize the usable space.

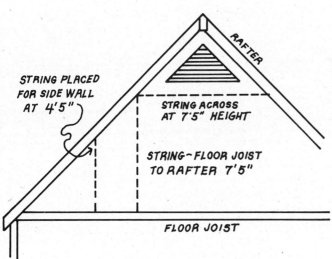

STRING PLACED FOR SIDE WALL AT 4'5"

RAFTER

STRING ACROSS AT 7'5" HEIGHT

STRING-FLOOR JOIST TO RAFTER 7'5"

FLOOR JOIST

Of course, all ceiling area in an attic does not have to be 7' high. Ceiling height along the side walls need be only 4' to 6' depending on use, such as sitting or sleeping. Determine how far back side walls can run, using strings to outline the backset. Allow for floor and ceiling sheet material thickness.

Note: Actual floor width will be less than this after side walls are built.

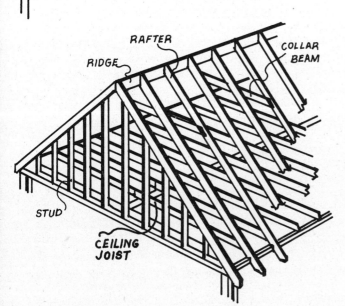

RIDGE

RAFTER

COLLAR BEAM

STUD

CEILING JOIST

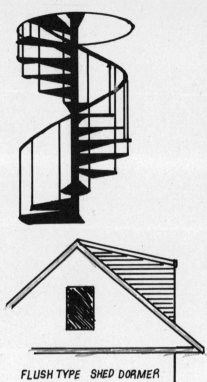

FLUSH TYPE SHED DORMER

RAFTERS ARE NOT CUT AND REMOVED UNTIL
ALL DORMER FRAMING IS CONSTRUCTED,
TIED TO THE PERMANENT MEMBERS AND
IS PROPERLY BRACED. A PROFESSIONAL SHOULD
BE CONTRACTED FOR THE DORMER FRAMING,
EXTERIOR SIDING AND THE ROOF SHEATHING.

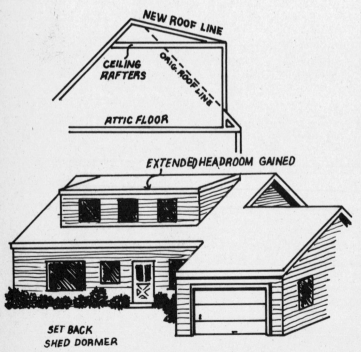

NEW ROOF LINE

CEILING
RAFTERS

ORIG. ROOF LINE

ATTIC FLOOR

EXTENDED HEADROOM GAINED

SET BACK
SHED DORMER

Another consideration is suitable access to the attic. Some homes have an adequate stairway to the area and only a "face lift" is needed. Others either have no access or the stairs are too narrow and steep for safe daily use. In this case, contact a knowledgeable carpenter or reputable home improvement contractor to do the stair work because specialized knowledge is required for the project. Ceiling and floor joists must be properly braced and supported when an opening is cut for the stairs. Also, a knowledgeable carpenter can determine just where the stair run should be installed and modified to fit available space.

DORMERS

If attic space is to be converted to usable living area, keep in mind that additional floor area and headroom can be gained by adding a dormer. This, of course, is not a job for the occasional handyman since it entails altering the roof line and roof structure. Since it is a fairly complicated project and can change the appearance of the front or rear of the house considerably, consider using a qualified professional familiar with this type of work.

What is a "dormer"? It is a means for reducing an existing roof pitch (slope) by raising a portion of that roof to form a different pitch ... thereby creating necessary height and width for installation of a vertical outside wall into which windows can be installed for light, ventilation and emergency exit.

There are basically two types of dormer ... flush to the gutter line or set back (up) from the gutter line. The dormer style should blend with the existing roof line.

A different approach combines the enlarged living area with a porch recessed in one side of the dormer.

90

A UNIQUE APPROACH TO A DORMER

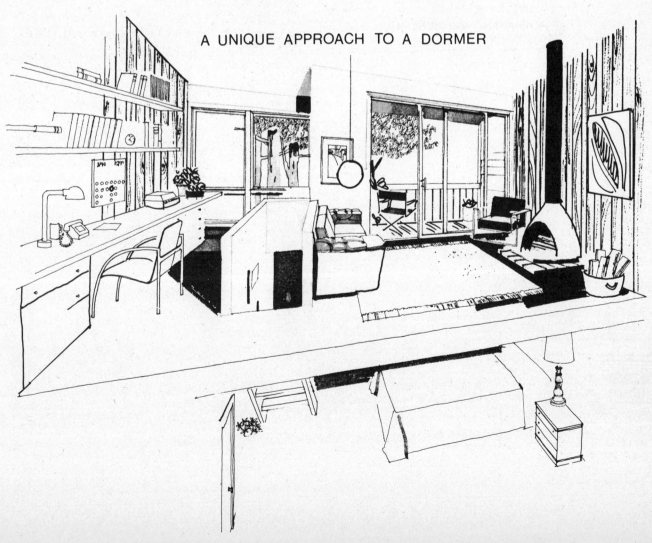

Many families need more room but are
not able to build an addition on because of local zoning restrictions.
The dormer project shown is well
suited for those post-war ranch houses
(and others constructed since) which
were built on narrow lots ... preclud-
ing any room additions.

This dormer extends the master bedroom
by utilizing the attic area as a study-
sitting room and is located directly over
the existing bedroom. It answers the
problem for parents living in modern-
size ranch homes who are losing "ground"
to their teenage children and friends.
The dormered room creates a private re-
treat of their own.

Access to the new area is by a stair-
ladder from the bedroom to the attic. The
cut-away illustration shows the relation
of the new attic expansion to the existing bedroom.

The new space offers a well lighted work
area, a modern wall-hung fireplace and an
attractive, railed deck for pleasant eve-
nings. This design created by G. Hugh
Tsuruoka for Georgia-Pacific Corporation
can be adapted to fit many ranch style
homes.

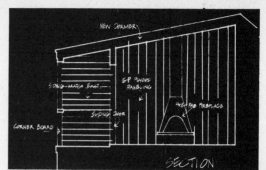

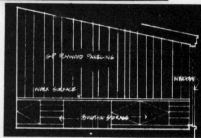

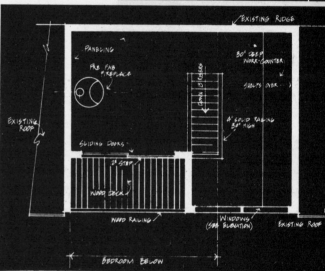

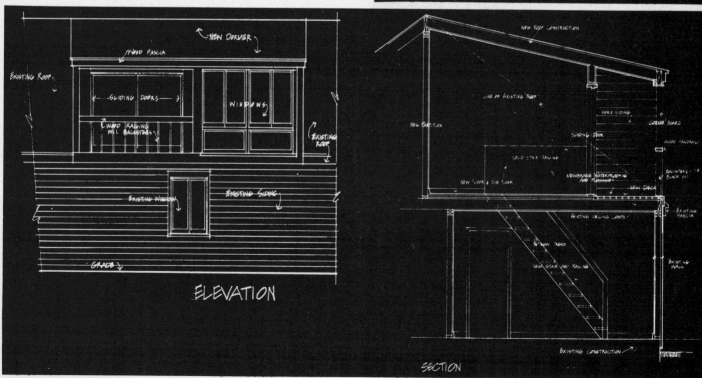

Courtesy of Georgia-Pacific Corporation

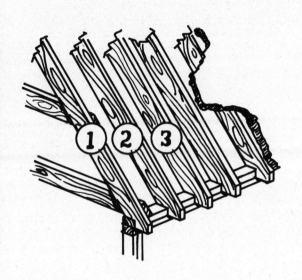

2. A minimum 7' clearance between the attic floor joists and the ridge beam which runs the length of the roof and to which all rafters tie to form the peak ... or, while maintaining the minimum allowable roof slope of 1" per foot drop, a 6'6" clearance is available between the floor joists and the proposed new attic ceiling joists.

3. The length of any proposed dormer should not extend beyond the third rafter from either end of the existing roof system. This is to maintain roof load strength and integrity.

4. Normally, a "truss" roof system (see carpentry glossary) is not adaptable to a dormer installation except by a qualified carpenter.

WILL A DORMER HELP?

To determine whether or not a dormer offers a practical solution to desired space requirements in an attic area, one can perform certain preliminary measurements.

> Caution: Before attempting any such measuring, safe walking surface should be in place to prevent an accidental slip that might damage the ceiling below.

1. Study the illustration ... note the original roof line and how it is changed by the addition of the dormer.

2. Measure the distance between the third rafters at either end of the attic. If all the space is not required for the planned room(s), mark those rafters which encompass the desired length.

3. From the point where the roof rafters tie into or run past the floor joists, measure at floor level four to six feet toward the middle of the attic. This can be a variable since it merely sets the height of the interior wall

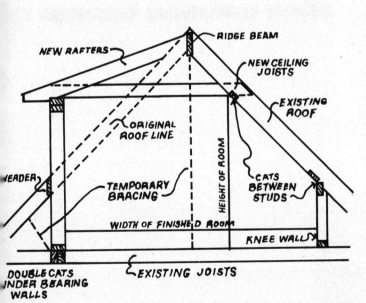

Certain conditions should exist for a dormer to be considered.

1. A stairway access to the attic.

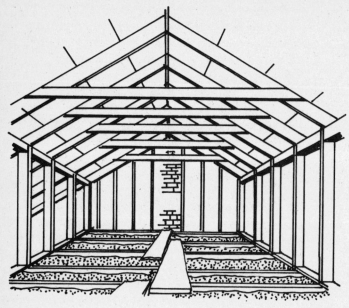

based on personal requirements and comfort. In other words, this wall might have a bed or other low furniture placed against it, so only four to five feet of headroom would be needed at the wall.

4. Repeat this measurement from the opposite side of the attic area. This will determine the height and location of the knee wall (see illustration).

5. Measure the desired length of the room, remembering to start at least 3 rafters in from the end. Using a chalk line, snap a line along the length of the room so that it intersects the measured point indicating the wall position (Step 3 above). Now visualize the effective size of the room which a dormer will create. The distance between the chalk lines will show the approximate width of the room. By slightly varying the knee-wall location, the appropriate dimensions of the room can be obtained.

FRAMING IN AN ATTIC

Framing in an attic consists of three basic parts: 1) side walls and ceiling joists; 2) endwall windows and ventilators; 3) partition walls. Install flooring before wall framing and ceiling joists. It is easier and also eliminates the possibility of accidentally punching a hole in the ceiling below.

STAPLE INSULATION   STUDS   CRIPPLES

SUB-FLOORING

Some homes have a ceiling-level exhaust fan. If the area in the attic is to be floored, the fan must be (a) moved to another location which will permit exhausting of the air flow or (b) disconnected at the switch so it cannot be accidentally turned on.

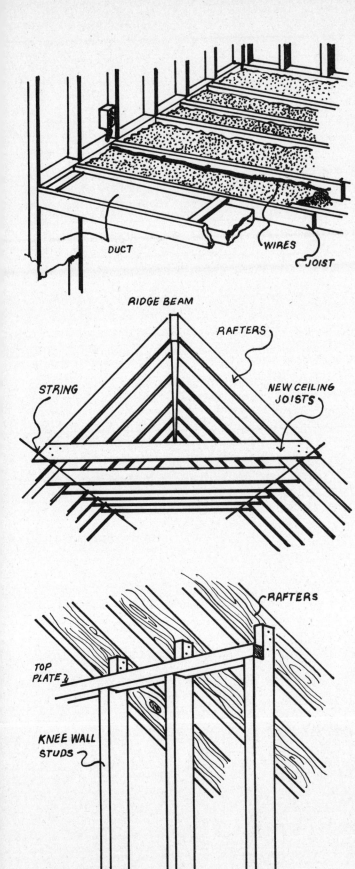

DUCT
WIRES
JOIST

RIDGE BEAM
RAFTERS
STRING
NEW CEILING JOISTS

RAFTERS
TOP PLATE
KNEE WALL STUDS
BOTTOM PLATE

1. Before installing flooring, make provisions for electrical circuits, plumbing runs and heating ducts. Leave old ceiling insulation in place. In cold climates, add insulation. It will act as a sound barrier to minimize noise penetration to the rooms below. Install flooring over complete area, well past where the side walls will be constructed. Even if area is not intended for storage, it can be used as a crawl space for routing electric circuits, plumbing runs, heat ducts and checking for roof leaks. Use 5/8" or 3/4" plywood for flooring on 16" o.c. joists. Any 24" o.c. joists should have 3/4" plywood or 1" planking. Plywood should extend to the rafters on each side, but not be fitted between them. This must remain open to maintain needed wall ventilation.

JOISTS

2. Ceiling joists should be installed next. Use 2 x 4's for joists up to 10'. Nail to rafters at each end using 12d nails. Be sure to level joists and nail at a uniform height above the floor to avoid ending up with a wavy ceiling. Tack a guide string at proper height between studs at each end. This will help maintain correct joist level.

SIDEWALLS

3. Next construct the sidewalls. There are several methods for building sidewalls, but the easiest to construct and attach is the prefabricated notched type. A 2 x 2" is used as a top plate ... a regular 2 x 4" for the bottom plate.

Studs are cut 5" over length so they extend past the top plate to allow nailing to the rafters. A notch 5" long and 2" deep is cut out of the top of each stud. Bottom plate and stud placement are layed out in standard 16" o.c. unless rafters are placed on 24" centers; then studs are placed 24" wide in each sidewall.

95

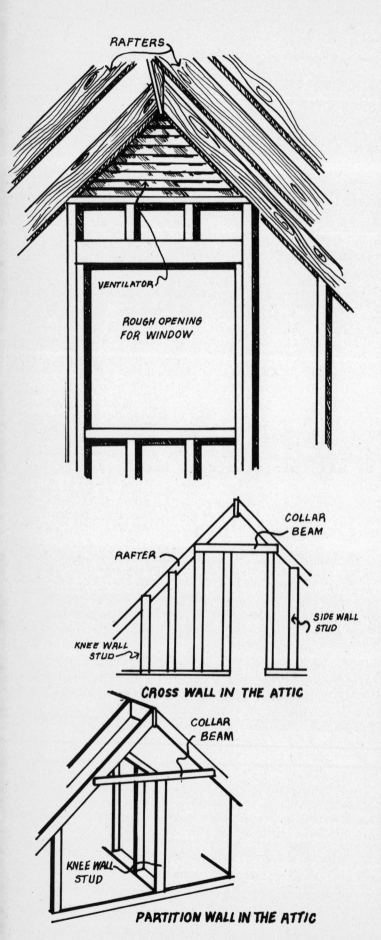

RAFTERS

VENTILATOR

ROUGH OPENING
FOR WINDOW

COLLAR
BEAM

RAFTER

SIDE WALL
STUD

KNEE WALL
STUD

CROSS WALL IN THE ATTIC

COLLAR
BEAM

KNEE WALL
STUD

PARTITION WALL IN THE ATTIC

When the sidewall has been constructed, raise into position,
level with shims and nail securely in position. The top is secured by nailing each stud
"extension" to a rafter. The
bottom is secured by nailing
through the bottom plate and into floor joists. Use 12d nails.

BLOCKING

An important step in sidewall
framing is nailing 2" x 2" or
2" x 4" blocking between rafters
and joists to act as a nailing
surface for sheathing panels.

END WALLS

End wall framing usually consists
of installing a window and possibly moving or modifying the ventilator. Do not close off any
ventilators. They are needed to
remove excess moisture in winter
and heat in summer. Most homes
have wedge-shaped ventilators located at the ridge or point of the
roof. These should be checked and
cleaned. Install new screen wire
on the inside to prevent entrance
of insects, squirrels and birds.
Be sure the ventilator base does
not extend below the top of the
new ceiling joists. If it does,
that portion should be blocked
off.

WINDOW FRAMING

4. The next step is framing for
windows ... done in much the same
way as in prefabed wall section.
The difference is that a temporary support for the ridgebeam
must be installed until the window header is in place. Measure
and mark the window opening and
framing locations on the end
wall sheathing and studs.

Before cutting any existing studs,
nail a 2 x 4 (or 2 x 6 for windows over 30" wide) above the
level the window opening is to be
cut. Cut a 2 x 4 to length and
nail in place under each end of
support. The support should be
nailed into all studs to be cut

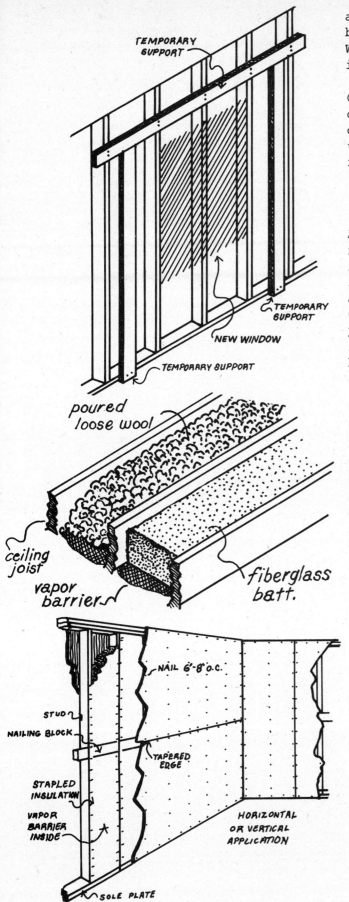

and extend 6" to one foot past both sides of the window opening. When the window frame has been installed, the support is removed.

One last point: A strong ladder or scaffolding is needed on the outside of the house when cutting through the opening and installing the window.

INSULATING THE ATTIC

After electric circuits, plumbing runs and heating ducts have been installed, the attic area must be insulated. The flat part of the attic ceiling should have at least 6" of batt-type insulation. Staple between joists with vapor barrier down ... or use pressure batts with a vapor barrier stapled to the underside of the joists.

The batt insulation thickness for the sloping portions of the ceiling depends on roof rafter dimensions. A clearance of 2" should be maintained between the roof sheathing and insulation to permit adequate ventilation of exterior house walls. Ideally, the rafters are 2 x 8's and 6" batt insulation can be used. With 2 x 6's, use 3 1/2" batts. Insulation should extend from edge of new ceiling joists to top of side wall. Staple to roof rafters, vapor barrier toward room.

Insulate the end and side walls, too, using 3 1/2" batt insulation on all walls, vapor barrier toward room. Insulation in end walls should extend up to new ceiling joists.

Garage conversion

PRELIMINARY CONSIDERATIONS

Home improvements which expand living space "above grade" usually add their full cost to the value of the house ... even when the job is contracted. When the homeowner does all or part of the work, the dollar gains can be significantly higher. "Above grade" means above ground level, and this type of improvement could involve a complete room addition or merely changing existing space into added living area. Two examples of this would be the enclosing of an open porch or converting a garage.

Converting an attached garage into a ground level family room, extra bedrooms, even a small "apartment" separated from the rest of the house can represent a worthwhile property investment. It can also add comfort and pleasure.

Some garages are finished to the degree that stud walls and ceiling joists have been covered over with a sheathing material, such as drywall, particle board or paneling ... others are unfinished. In either case, certain construction deficiencies might exist. The two most common are: (a) undersized ceiling joists and wall studs and (b) excessive spacing between joists or studs. Both can usually be corrected.

FLOORS

Nearly all garages have a slab concrete floor, and this has a bearing on the type of improved floor that can be considered. Climate restricts the choice to some extent. In the South, vinyl or vinyl asbestos tile could be applied directly to the concrete. In northern climates, some sort of insulation would be required to keep heating costs within reason.

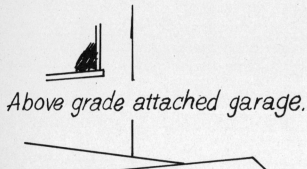

Above grade attached garage.

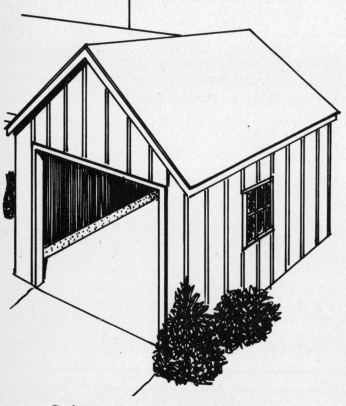

Ceiling joists may be undersize.

Wall studs may be set too wide.

Concrete slab could need insulating.

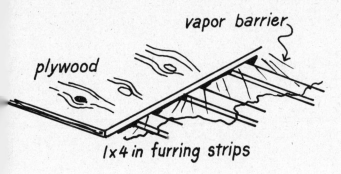

plywood

vapor barrier

1x4 in furring strips

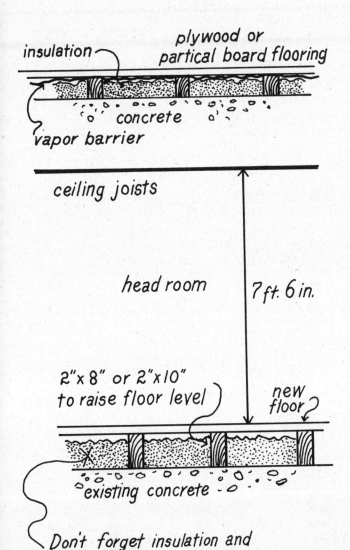

insulation

plywood or
partical board flooring

concrete

vapor barrier

ceiling joists

head room   7 ft. 6 in.

2"x 8" or 2"x10"
to raise floor level

new
floor

existing concrete

Don't forget insulation and
vapor barrier.

Several alternatives are well worth considering:

1. Installing 1" x 4" furring boards over the concrete. This is covered with a polyethylene vapor barrier and an exterior grade plywood. The surface could then be covered with tile, linoleum or carpeting material.

2. Place 2 x 4's on edge to act as "shallow" floor joists. This would permit the installation of adequate insulation to assure a warm floor. The vapor barrier and exterior grade plywood would be fastened to the 2 x 4's. Spacing, of course, would be 16" o.c.

3. The most expensive method involves raising the entire floor area to match the level of existing floors in the house. Increased cost is due to the lumber requirements for these floor joists ... 2 x 8's, 2 x 10's or larger. A limiting factor is the resulting loss of headroom when both the floor and ceiling are finished.

HEAT

Heat for the new room is a key consideration. Before starting any work, investigate carefully the options available that can produce safe and comfortable heat ... and cooling. Two possibilities are:

1. <u>Existing Forced Air, Steam or Hot Water</u>. Can the present system handle, or be modified to handle, the added load requirements? Evaluating the system is a job for an expert because overtaxing the capacity limits of a furnace can lead to premature replacement of expensive parts. A recognized heating contractor is also recommended for any work involved with installing duct work or pipes.

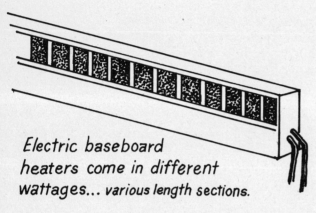

Electric baseboard heaters come in different wattages... various length sections.

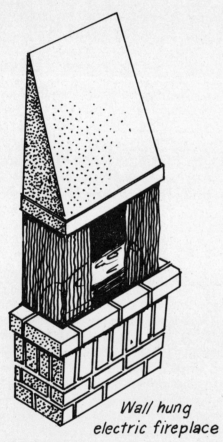

Wall hung electric fireplace

2. <u>Supplemental Heating System.</u> Electrical baseboard, space heater or wall-hung decorative fireplace with a blower can sometimes serve heating requirements and prove less expensive to install since much of the work can be done by the owner. A further savings can be realized when a thermostat is installed. With this device, temperatures can be controlled ... when the room is not in use, set the thermostat to 50-60 degrees; increase it to a comfortable level when it is going to be used.

<u>Note</u>: Electrical supplementary heat is suggested for two reasons ... safety, and the fact that natural gas is and may continue to be in restricted supply, even in geographical areas which heretofore had plenty.

Regardless of the heating and cooling method selected, operating costs will be reduced substantially when the ceiling, walls and floor are correctly insulated. Storm windows and doors should be considered for the same reason.

INSTALLING ADDITIONAL
CEILING JOISTS

Local building codes should be carefully checked whenever an area not originally intended for living is to be converted into a room. The code will specify framing and other construction requirements such as for windows, doors, joists and any restrictions which must be observed.

Under normal circumstances, 2 x 6 joists on 24" centers can be used in a one-car attached garage; however, 16" centers will result in a stronger finished ceiling and fewer problems over the years.

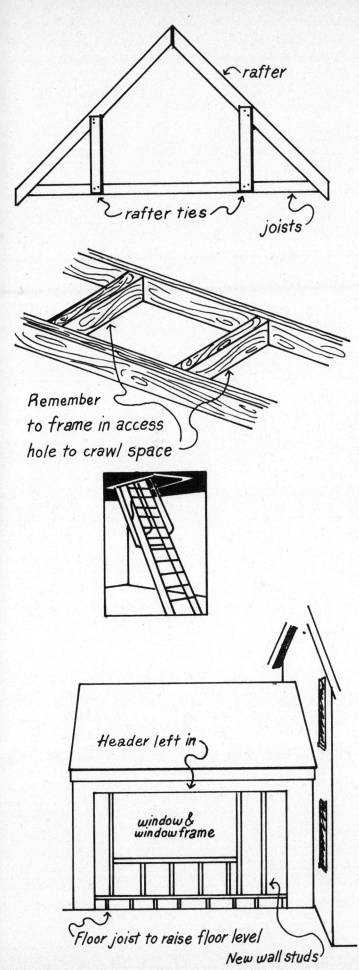

rafter

rafter ties

joists

Remember
to frame in access
hole to crawl space

Header left in

window &
window frame

Floor joist to raise floor level

New wall studs

Joists spanning a two-car garage without a center support beam and column should also utilize 2 x 6's plus two rafter ties. These should be nailed to the joists and respective rafters about one-third from each end. Where 2 x 8 joists are used, a single tie can be fastened between joists and rafters or to the center ridge beam.

Joists spanning a two-car garage with a center support beam and column can be 2 x 4's with 1 x 4 rafter tie nailed at the midway point. With 2 x 4's, always set on 16" centers to prevent sagging, popping of drywall nails and cracking.

Remember to frame in an access hole to the crawl space to assure entrance for checking electrical wiring, pipes or possible roof leaks. Access can be gained by either an installed pull-down stairway or simply a ladder when needed. It is a good idea to lay in sufficient plywood sheets or planking to serve as a partial floor in the crawl space before adding drywall to the ceiling.

Note: Attic crawl space should not be used for storage if joists are set on 24" centers. Where ceilings have 24" joist spacing, use 5/8" drywall ... anything less may not provide the strength and rigidity to span two feet without some ultimate sagging.

ENCLOSING A
GARAGE DOOR OPENING

To enclose the opening where a garage door is to be removed, a standard stud wall is built to fit the space. A direct type installation is suggested in order to achieve a good fit and to facilitate the framing of windows and doors. However, if a solid wall is planned, then the prefab method might prove easier for the individual working alone.

101

TO AVOID A FUTURE ANNOYANCE WHEN
TRYING TO ANCHOR DRAPERY RODS,
ADD BLOCKING BETWEEN STUDS ON BOTH
SIDES OF WINDOW FRAMING. POSITION
SO THE TOP EDGES OF THE BLOCKS ARE
LEVEL WITH THE BOTTOM EDGE OF THE HEADER.

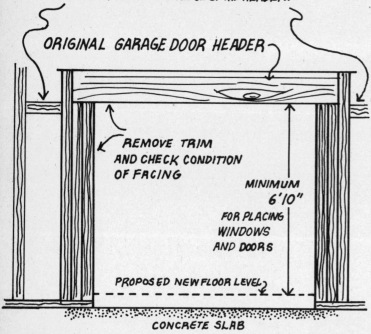

ORIGINAL GARAGE DOOR HEADER

REMOVE TRIM
AND CHECK CONDITION
OF FACING

MINIMUM
6'10"

FOR PLACING
WINDOWS
AND DOORS

PROPOSED NEW FLOOR LEVEL

CONCRETE SLAB

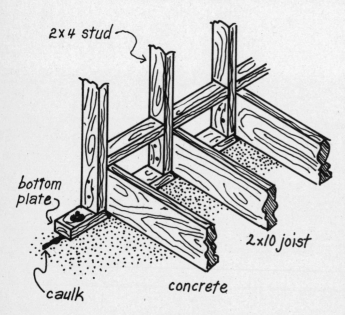

2x4 stud

bottom
plate

2x10 joist

caulk

concrete

There is a large header above the existing door opening. This should not be removed. Instead, utilize this oversized header for installing a picture window, sliding glass door or one or more standard windows.

1. Remove the door, any tracking and bracing as well as trim around the opening ... both inside and out. At this point, check the condition of the facing boards on the sides and top of the opening. If they are in good condition ... without dry rot, cracks or splits ... wall framing can be nailed through these facing boards into the studs behind.

2. Measure clearance from the top facing board to the concrete and subtract thickness of the planned floor. Will leaving the facing board in seriously affect clearance for doors and windows? The rough-in height for each is 6'10" above the finished floor. If necessary, remove the facing board.

3. Measure, cut and install the bottom plate, securing it to the concrete slab with either concrete nails, anchor bolts, stud gun or waterproofed adhesive. To avoid a potential problem from rot, use either redwood 2 x 4's or standard pine studs treated with a rot and termite inhibitor.

Except when using an adhesive, lay a solid band of caulk on the underside of the bottom plate to block potential seepage. Use a caulk that is guaranteed to remain pliable and NOT one that will become hard and brittle. Tap the plate soundly along its length to spread the caulk.

4. Measure stud lengths to fit framed opening ... remember to include the framing members for windows and doors. Construct the wall, toenailing the studs when they have been plumbed to position on 16" centers.

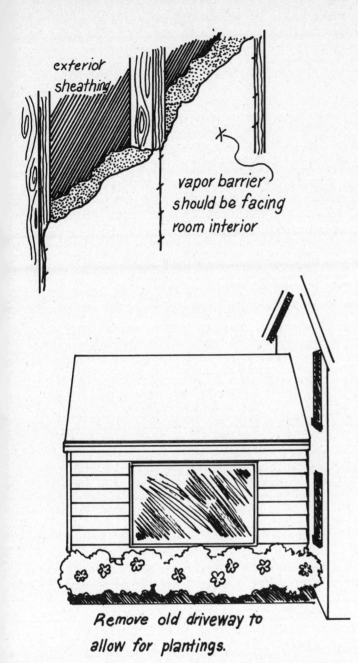

exterior sheathing

vapor barrier should be facing room interior

Remove old driveway to allow for plantings.

Have enough polyethylene to tack over the opening should construction be delayed for any reason. If tools and materials are to be left inside the garage area, consider a black polyethylene so the interior is not visible.

5. Staple insulation with the vapor barrier facing the room interior. Stuff scrap pieces into all openings and around the door and window framing. Add an extra bead of caulk along the bottom plate ... both inside and out.

6. Installation of drywall in both walls and ceiling should not be undertaken until all rough-in work has been completed, including flooring. Exterior finish is not detailed because of the many types of exterior sheathing which might be used ... brick veneer, stone, shingles, plywood with battened strips, wood or aluminum siding, etc. Each requires a degree of skill that recommends contracting for this portion of the garage improvement. It may be desirable to contract for a professional to break up and remove all or part of the driveway or apron in front of the finished wall addition to permit plantings to compliment the overall appearance.

RAISING GARAGE FLOORS

FURRING STRIP METHOD

How far above the concrete surface should the new floor level be raised? If merely enough to gain air space insulation from the concrete and allow for level installation of a sub-floor and floor covering, then 1 x 3, 1 x 4 or 2 x 4 furring strips can be used.

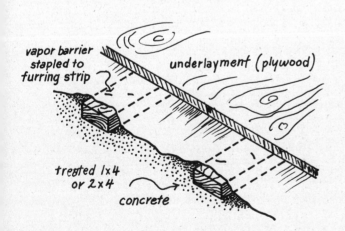

vapor barrier stapled to furring strip

underlayment (plywood)

treated 1x4 or 2x4

concrete

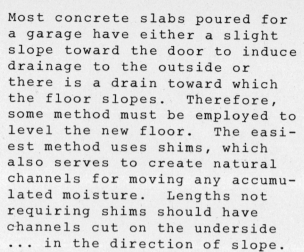

shims allow for
moisture drainage

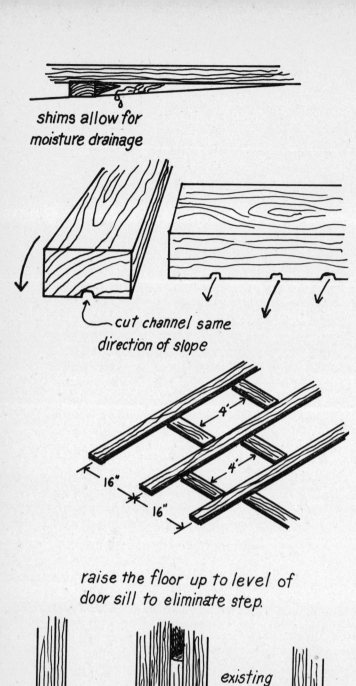

cut channel same
direction of slope

16"
4'
16"
4'

raise the floor up to level of
door sill to eliminate step.

existing
door

subfloor

2x8 joist

concrete

Most concrete slabs poured for a garage have either a slight slope toward the door to induce drainage to the outside or there is a drain toward which the floor slopes. Therefore, some method must be employed to level the new floor. The easiest method uses shims, which also serves to create natural channels for moving any accumulated moisture. Lengths not requiring shims should have channels cut on the underside ... in the direction of slope.

Where moisture might be a problem, seal the floor with a concrete sealant. Then, a network of furring boards are laid on 16" centers with cross pieces set each 4 ft. A 4-mil polyethylene vapor barrier is now laid over the furring and stapled enough to hold it in place. The sub-floor can be nailed in place and the final cover ... carpet, tile, linoleum, etc. ... installed.

The use of 2 x 4 lumber set on edge allows room for a good insulator. A 3" batt with vapor barrier can be stapled to the 2 x 4's. A safety precaution for concrete floors subject to moisture build-up is to lay a 4-mil polyethylene directly over the concrete before installing the 2 x 4 furrings 16" o.c. Cross bracing should be nailed every 4 ft. Fiberglass insulation with a vapor barrier is stapled between the members with the barrier up ... towards the room.

STANDARD JOIST METHOD

Raising A Floor Level Up To Eight Inches

To raise the new floor level up enough to match adjacent rooms or provide a shallow step down, 2 x 6's or 2 x 8's can solve the problem. The technique is similar to building a stud wall section except that joist headers serve the functions of top and bottom plates.

104

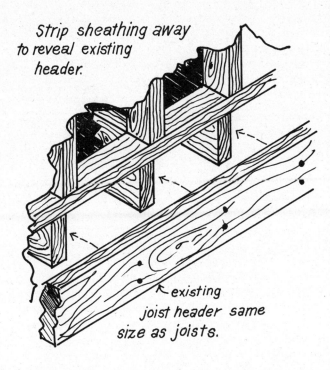

Strip sheathing away to reveal existing header.

existing joist header same size as joists.

Joist headers are the same size as the joists to be used. They are nailed to studs along the base length of the wall opposite the house structure. A joist header is already in place in the common wall. This is exposed by removing the sheathing at the base of the wall.

To install joist headers and joists, follow these steps:

1. Determine the surface (actual) lumber size which comes closest to the needed elevation. Do this by measuring from the top of the existing joist header in the common wall to the surface of the concrete floor and matching this figure to actual lumber dimensions. It should be less, not more, because minor adjustments can be made with furring or the addition of a second layer of subflooring to bring it even.

2. Using the top of the existing joist header in the common wall, snap a chalk line this identical height on the perimeter stud walls. Check frequently that the line is running absolutely _level_ because this will establish the height of both the joist header on the wall opposite the common wall and the outside joists on the side walls.

3. Measure and cut the required lengths of lumber for the new joist header and carefully nail it in position with the top even with the chalk line. Drive at least two 16d nails into alternate studs and one into each intermediate stud. If more than one length of lumber is needed, install the full length piece first; then, measure, cut and nail the shorter piece in place. Be sure the butt end is tight.

4. Measure and cut the first joist length, position even with the chalk line on the side wall studs and nail; add any additional length needed as described for the joist header. Repeat this step on the

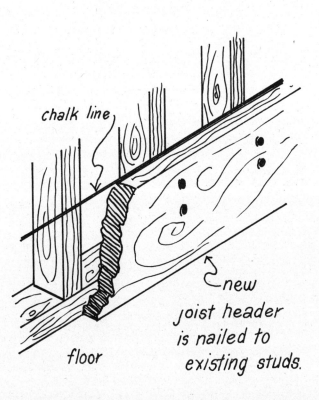

chalk line

floor

new joist header is nailed to existing studs.

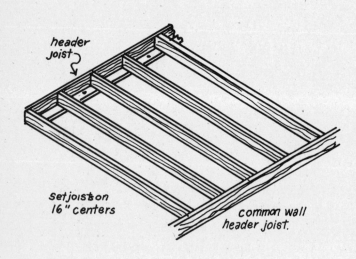

header joist

Set joist on 16" centers

common wall header joist.

opposite side wall. At this point the entire perimeter has joist lumber securely fastened to each stud wall at the chalk line. The next step is the measuring, cutting and positioning of the first interior joist.

5. Floor joists are usually placed perpendicular to the common wall to permit heating ducts, water pipes and electrical wiring to run between rather than through joist members. They are set on 16" centers, starting from either side wall. The next step is the measuring, cutting and positioning of the first interior joist. Place it in position but do not nail.

6. With the aid of another pair of hands, stretch a chalkline along the length of the positioned joist to help locate high and low spots. This step is very important to assure a level floor surface ... one that doesn't squeak underfoot. If high spots of more than one-eighth of an inch are apparent, the joist should be flipped over, thus converting the high spot to a low. Shims are used to raise it to the correct level. This must be done with each intermediate joist before subflooring is laid in place.

7. When the joists are in final position, toenail each end to its header using at least two 12d nails on each side. Re-stretch the chalkline and drive shims under those joists where low spots occur ... bringing them flush with the chalk line. Now check that there is no space greater than 3 feet between any two shims. Where this occurs, fit additional shims in place but do not force them, as their sole function is to prevent the joist from sagging. Do this for each joist, in turn.

8. Insulated heat ducts, wrapped water pipes and electrical wiring are installed before the subflooring is laid and nailed. A useful trick sometimes employed by experienced remodelers is to run

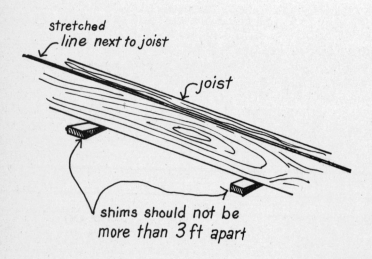

stretched line next to joist

joist

shims should not be more than 3 ft apart

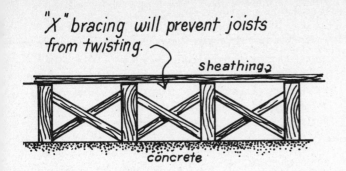

"X" bracing will prevent joists from twisting.

sheathing

concrete

everything between the same two joists. Then, a 16" wide trap door is cut from the subflooring to permit later access without having to remove full sheets. This is easy to do when the ducts etc. are run near a wall. Also, "X" bracing is recommended to hold joists in true alignment and prevent twisting.

Raising A Floor Level More Than Eight Inches

Actually, a floor level can be raised more than eight inches with the use of large dimensional lumber ... 2 x 12's and even 2 x 14's. However, lumber this size commands premium prices, so another technique is employed to raise floor levels more than eight inches. It uses a ledger board and beam.

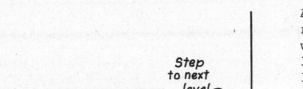

Step to next level

2 x 12
2 x 8
2 x 4

OLD FLOOR LEVEL

A ledger board and beam installation differs from the joist on-floor method. First, as the name suggests, a ledger board is installed on common and opposite walls at a predetermined height. With the joist resting on the ledge at each end, the desired elevation for the floor is obtained. Second, a beam is installed midway between the joist headers. This is built up the amount required to bring the top even with the tops of the ledger boards. The beam carries a portion of the weight load, thus taking some of the strain that would occur in the middle of the span.

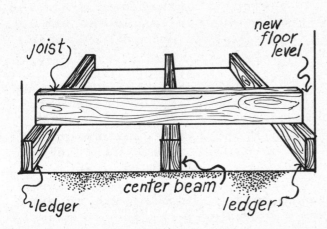

joist

new floor level

center beam

ledger   ledger

FLOOR JOIST & RAFTER SIZING

50 POUNDS PER SQURE FOOT - LIVE LOAD			60 POUNDS PER SQUARE FOOT - LIVE LOAD		
JOIST SIZE	MAXIMUM SPAN ON 12" CENTERS	MAXIMUM SPAN ON 16" CENTERS	JOIST SIZE	MAXIMUM SPAN ON 12" CENTERS	MAXIMUM SPAN ON 16" CENTERS
2 X 6	8'·6" TO 10'·0"	7'·9" TO 9'·1"	2 X 6	8'·1" TO 9'·6"	7'·4" TO 8'·7"
2 X 8	11'·4" TO 13'·3"	10'·4" TO 12'·1"	2 X 8	10'·9" TO 12'·7"	9'·9" TO 11'·5"
2 X 10	14'·3" TO 16'·8"	13'·0" TO 15'·3"	2 X 10	13'·6" TO 15'·10"	12'·4" TO 14'·6"
2 X 12	17'·2" TO 20'·1"	15'·9" TO 18'·5"	2 X 12	16'·4" TO 19'·1"	14'·11" TO 17'·5"
2 X 14	20'·1" TO 23'·6"	18'·5" TO 21'·6"	2 X 14	19'·1" TO 22'·4"	17'·6" TO 20'·5"

If a center beam is to be used, use the span of beam to footing.

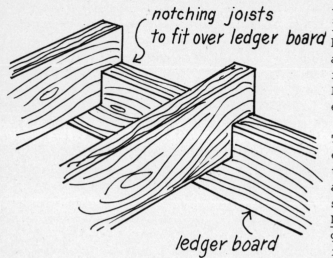

notching joists
to fit over ledger board

ledger board

Since the joists will not rest on the floor, shims cannot be used for leveling. Additionally, the lumber selected for the joist must be at least 2 x 8 to support the floor loads across the open span. Refer to the chart for recommended joist dimensions.

There are two methods which can be employed with the ledger board technique. One employs notching at bottom corner of each joist end so the notch fits around the ledge. Note: Using this method, the ledger board will have to be raised in direct proportion to the depth of the notch in order to bring the finished floor up to desired height.

The second, more common technique used for floor joist, requires the use of a larger lumber size for the ledger but notching is not necessary ... the bottom edge of the joist rests on the ledger and is nailed into that position. The notching method is time consuming; therefore, the method explained here is the second.

To install a ledger board and beam joist system, follow these steps:

1. Mark and chalk line around the perimeter walls the exact height for the top of joists when installed. Check for level, and make sure the chalk line snapped on the common wall is met exactly by the chalk line on the third wall.

2. Measure the actual depth of the joist to be used and mark from the first chalk line the depth of the joist at several points on the common wall. Again snap a chalk line, making sure it is level. Continue this line around the perimeter walls. This line will position the top edge of the ledger board, when installed.

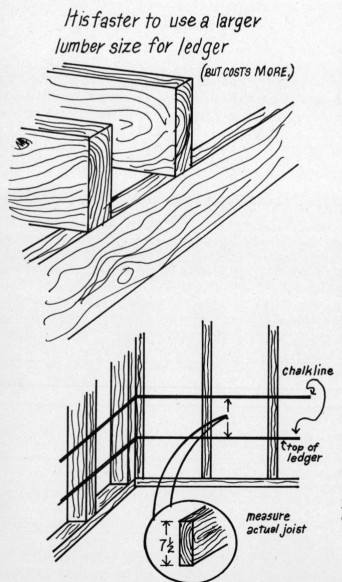

It is faster to use a larger lumber size for ledger
(BUT COSTS MORE.)

chalkline

top of ledger

measure actual joist

7½

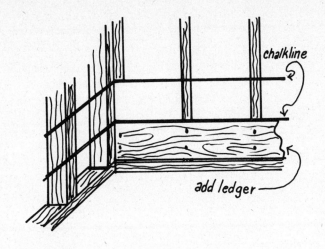

chalkline

add ledger

3. The next step is to determine the size of the ledger board needed for the job. Do this by measuring from the lower chalk line to the floor. If it measures less than the lumber selected for the joist, use the appropriate standard size 2 x ? lumber that will allow the ledger to rest on the concrete floor. If, on the other hand, the distance is greater, the ledger board is nailed in place to the studs above the floor surface ... and the joists will have to be notched.

4. Measure, cut and nail the ledger board in position on the common wall header so the top is flush with the lower chalk line. Nail it securely ... use two 12d nails every 16" along the length. Repeat the same steps for the wall opposite the common wall.

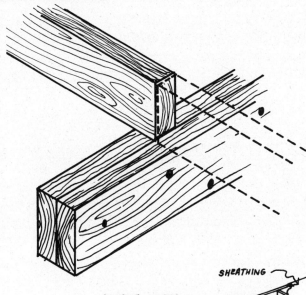

5. The beam is next. A double beam is often worthwhile for the extra strength it offers. A double beam is merely nailing two identical pieces together. This is a "must" where joists will abutt at the beam.

The top of the beam must be brought to the same level as the top of the ledger boards in order to have a level floor surface. Therefore, stretch two strings an equal distance from the two side walls and tack the ends at the ledger board chalk lines. This is the height the beam must reach. Use shims to adjust, and make sure it is level. When properly positioned, nail it in place to the side walls. Remember ... the beam will run parallel to the common wall midway between the common wall and the opposite wall. It is nailed to wall studs at each end.

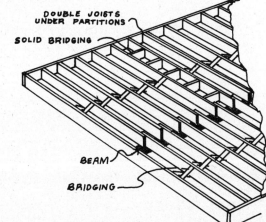

SHEATHING

DOUBLE JOISTS UNDER PARTITIONS

SOLID BRIDGING

BEAM

BRIDGING

6. Cut the first joist to length and position along a side wall. The ends should rest on the ledger boards. Nail directly to each stud, using two 12d nails. Repeat this part of the installation with a joist nailed in position along the opposite side wall.

109

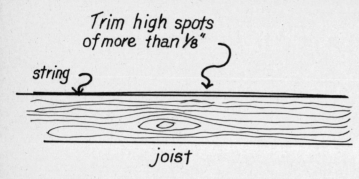

Trim high spots
of more than ⅛"

string

joist

7. Cut an intermediate joist to length and position it on the ledger board and beam. Stretch a chalk line along the length of the joist to help detect high and low spots. Where a low spot is noted, flip the joist over so the low spot becomes a high spot. Note: This is exactly opposite of the procedure followed when joists rest on the floor. Therefore, high spots greater than 1/8" every four feet of span should be either trimmed to size or not used as a full-length joist. High spots less than 1/8" generally straighten out when subflooring is nailed in place. Toenail the joists to the ledger boards at each end and the center beam.

8. Re-check height of the joists with strings. Make any adjustments necessary ... now!

9. The ledger and beam system does not provide a nailing surface at the joist ends. Therefore, this is added before subflooring. The least expensive approach is to cut scrap 2 x 4 lumber to size ... so it fits between the joists. Note the illustration. Either butt nail through the joists into the blocks or toenail through the block into the joists.

10. Add "X" bracing as previously described.

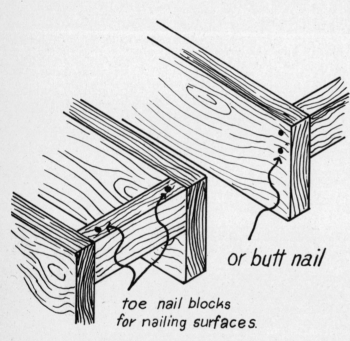

or butt nail

toe nail blocks
for nailing surfaces.

PLANNING
A ROOM ADDITION

When a home does not have available space in the basement, garage, attic or porch for expanding living area, an addition to the existing house might be the answer. Several things must be considered and a certain amount of investigation is necessary.

Zoning restrictions must be checked for your specific location. A defined setback is required, and this may preclude building any addition toward the street. Easements to the side or back of the property line are also spelled out, so investigate carefully.

A plat of your property will show legal property lines, fences, permanent landscape, walks and drives and house position in relation to boundaries. Where do you find the plat? Mortgage papers or the original architect's drawings may include the plat. In any event, one is generally required by zoning boards when applying for a property modification; also the building department will want a copy when a construction permit request is filed. You may have to order a special survey by a licensed surveyor.

Utilities have permanent easements, usually underground, and these include water, gas, electrical and sewer lines. You cannot build over these. If you have any doubt as to exact locations, the respective utility should be able to provide the necessary information. Incidentally, the cost for moving any meter, power lines, etc. is normally charged to the property owner.

Another consideration is the "lay of the land." Land fill and leveling can be expensive. Merely getting it to the place needed might also entail damage to established lawn and landscaping. It will help to select a level area where grading costs can be held to a minimum.

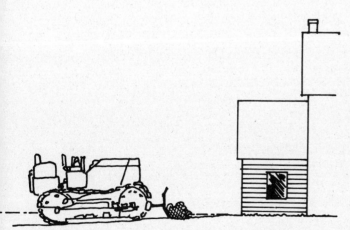

property line

addition shaded

existing house

ft.

setback as required by local code restrictions

ft.

drive

sewer

water turn off

city easement

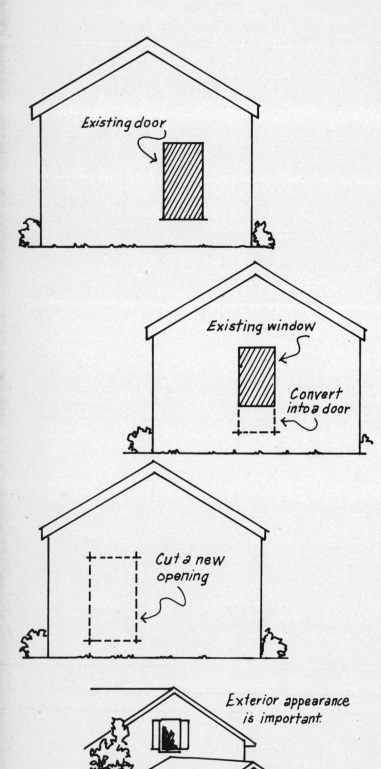

Square footage of the room addition must be determined early in the planning to assure conformance to building code restrictions.

Another consideration is assuring a convenient entrance to the new room. Entry can be gained in several ways:

1. An existing door that is suitably located to serve the new room.

2. An existing window which can be converted into a door or open walk-through.

3. Cutting a new opening through the exterior wall of the house to create an entrance.

The first represents the "easy" way. The second is more work but not too difficult. Three is more complicated; to open a hole in a bearing exterior wall, adequate bracing must be installed to carry the weight load while the opening is being framed. It is a job best left to a professional carpenter or builder.

Where an existing door is used, be sure to check your fire code ... it may require a door from the new room so the total number of exits from the house remains the same.

Exterior appearance of the addition certainly warrants careful thought. You want it to blend in with the house so it looks like it was "always there." The material used to finish the exterior can match the rest of the house or not ... this is a personal choice ... but it cannot detract from the surrounding neighborhood.

Windows should be sized and located in balance with the rest of the house while providing ample light, ventilation and wall area for comfortable furniture placement.

CONVERTING A WINDOW INTO A DOOR

The first step in converting a window into a door is determining the existing floor level. The method shown can be used to determine floor level at that window.

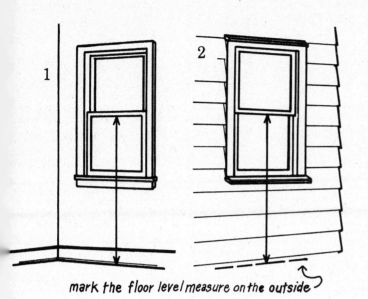

mark the floor level measure on the outside

1. On the inside of the window, measure down from a convenient point on the window to the floor level. Then, on the outside of the house, measure down that distance from the same point on the window and mark the siding. This indicates the distance off the ground the door will be. If for access to a patio area, steps may be necessary unless the grade level is to be changed. Be sure to order a pre-hung <u>exterior</u> door which includes the threshold.

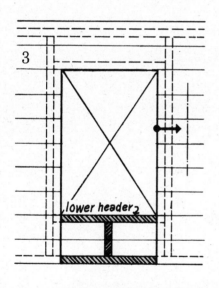

lower header

2. Remove the casing, sill and window; measure the opening for the door size that can be accommodated. The extent of the window framing can be found by driving nails through the siding at several locations.

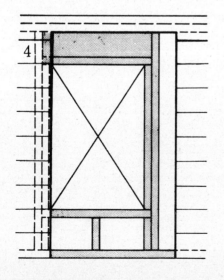

3. If the rough window opening is 6'10" high and wide enough to accept the desired size door, remove the interior and exterior sheathing below the window and the lower header and cripple (drawing #3). To install the new door, see instructions for pre-hung doors.

4. If the opening must be made wider to accommodate the desired door, remove the sheathing to the rough-in size required, install temporary roof support bracing and remove the shaded framing members.

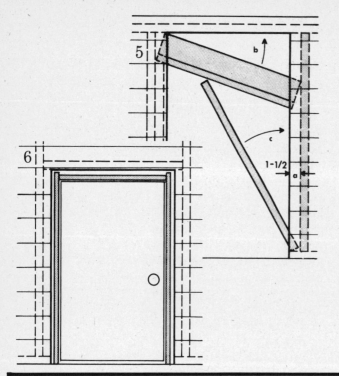

5. Install new framing as follows:
(a) Recess the stud 1 1/2" back
from the opening and behind the
siding. Toenail into the top and
bottom plates; (b) Hold the header
in place by temporarily nailing
through the siding; (c) Set the
cripple into place, nailing directly into the stud and toenail
into the header.

6. Remove the temporary roof bracing and install the new pre-hung
door.

When the window conversion to a door
is for access to a patio or similar
use, stairs may be required. Quite
frequently the door sill will end
up above grade level.

Two or three alternates are available:

1. Build wooden steps using a wea-
ther-resistant lumber such as
plywood.

2. Build forms and pour concrete
steps ... with or without a stoop.

3. Install pre-cast concrete steps
... with or without a stoop.

Pre-cast steps may well be the easy
way for the homeowner to complete
the job in a morning or afternoon.

Pre-cast steps are usually rein-
forced with metal bar. Stair treads
come 10 or 12 inches deep; the riser, 6 to 8 inches. A stoop will
be about 24 inches deep ... without
it you merely have a top step.
Over-all widths run 3 and 4 feet.
Footings are generally not necessary because they are heavy enough
to stay in place ... roughly 100 lb.
per step, and a stoop will add to
this.

To prevent any settling, several 8
x 16 inch concrete blocks can be
buried flush to ground level along
the house foundation. These will
pick up the weight at the back ...
where most of it is located.

An optional decorative wrought iron
railing can be installed. Only a
variable speed drill, masonry bit
and matching lead anchors and bolts
will be needed.

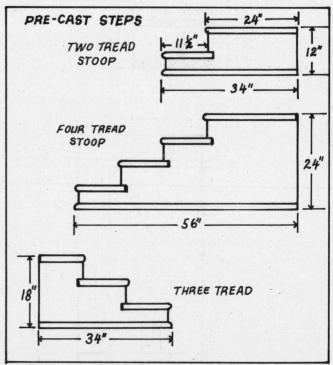

TYPICAL ROOM ADDITION

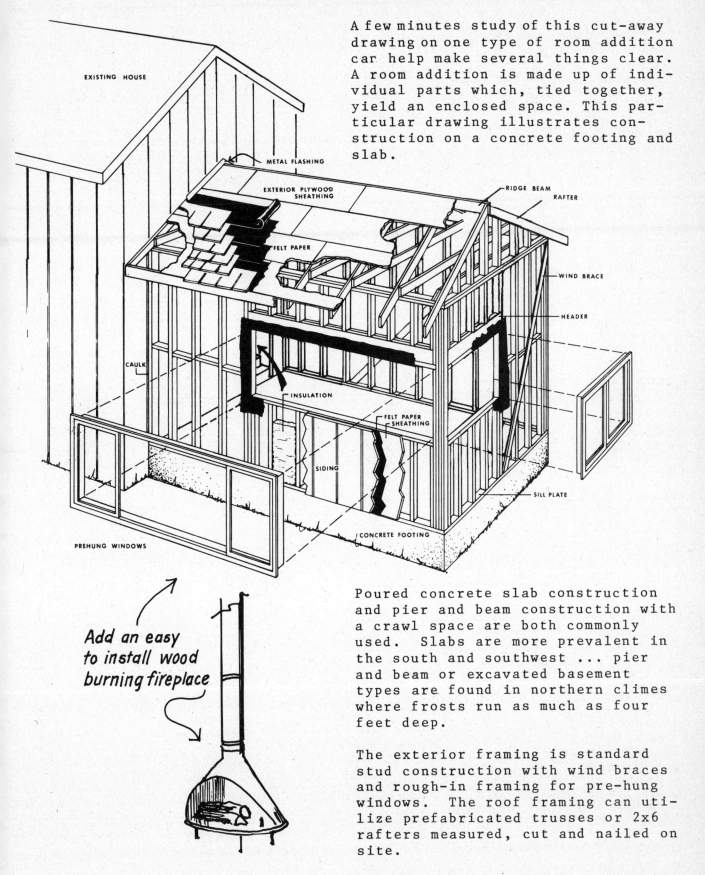

EXISTING HOUSE

METAL FLASHING

EXTERIOR PLYWOOD SHEATHING

RIDGE BEAM

RAFTER

FELT PAPER

WIND BRACE

HEADER

CAULK

INSULATION

FELT PAPER SHEATHING

SIDING

SILL PLATE

PREHUNG WINDOWS

CONCRETE FOOTING

Add an easy to install wood burning fireplace

A few minutes study of this cut-away drawing on one type of room addition car help make several things clear. A room addition is made up of individual parts which, tied together, yield an enclosed space. This particular drawing illustrates construction on a concrete footing and slab.

Poured concrete slab construction and pier and beam construction with a crawl space are both commonly used. Slabs are more prevalent in the south and southwest ... pier and beam or excavated basement types are found in northern climes where frosts run as much as four feet deep.

The exterior framing is standard stud construction with wind braces and rough-in framing for pre-hung windows. The roof framing can utilize prefabricated trusses or 2x6 rafters measured, cut and nailed on site.

The roof is finished with plywood sheathing, felt paper and shingles.

Note that the plywood sheets are laid out so the joints are staggered. Where the roof joins the house, metal flashing is installed with the bottom edge between the felt paper and the shingles.

Where the walls of the addition tie into the wall of the existing house the joints are caulked. Side walls are enclosed with plywood or insulation board, felt paper and the exterior finish which might be wood, metal or fiberglass siding, shingles, brick veneer, stucco, etc.

FOOTING TRENCH LAYOUT

CONCRETE MIX CHART

WHERE USED	CU. FT. SAND	CU.FT.GRAVEL	BAGS CEMENT	GALS. WATER
FLOORS·STEPS·WALKS OVER 2"THK.	2-1/4	3	1	5
FOOTINGS·FOUNDATION WALLS	2-3/4	4	1	5-1/2
TWO COURSE FLOORS·BENCHES·CONCRETE LESS THAN 2" THICK	1-3/4	2-1/4	1	4
CONCRETE BLOCK MORTAR	6	0	1	5

Eight stakes, four 1x4 batter boards, five lengths of heavy string and a weight for each end, a tape measure and level are the requirements for laying out and squaring the foundation wall for a room addition. The illustration shows the setup.

Stakes are first driven along the foundation of the house, spaced to the width of the addition to be built. The batter boards are put in place and string lengths with a weight at each end are placed over the batter boards from the stakes at the house. Another runs between the two batter boards. The strings are moved until they form the outline of the exterior of the proposed foundation wall.

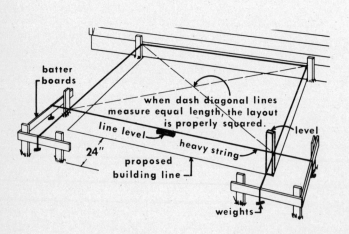

batter boards
when dash diagonal lines measure equal length, the layout is properly squared.
line level
level
24"
heavy string
proposed building line
weights

Diagonal strings are then used to square the outline. The weighted strings are easy to adjust. With everything squared, drive an extra stake at each outside corner where the diagonals intersect the perimeter strings.

The horizontal level is set with the line level. This establishes the height to which the foundation will be built. See the illustration of the concrete block buildup.

Excavation of the trench is heavy work and you may choose to hire it done. There may be certain contractors who are reluctant to take on just a small portion of the job but small companies are often very willing to let you subcontract the work.

REINFORCED CONCRETE FOOTINGS, FOUNDATION AND SLAB

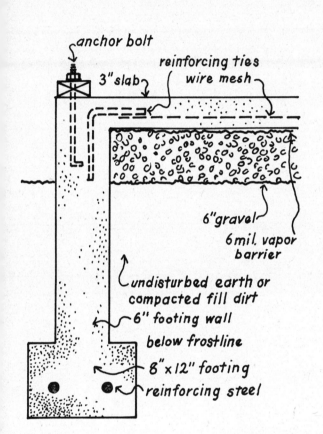

anchor bolt

reinforcing ties
wire mesh

3" slab

6" gravel

6 mil. vapor barrier

undisturbed earth or compacted fill dirt

6" footing wall
below frostline

8"x12" footing

reinforcing steel

This section-thru view of a typical 8"x12" footing and poured concrete foundation shows steel bar reinforcements as well as the steel mesh laid within the slab. Local building codes usually specify footing size and depth as well as the proper aggregate mix suitable for local soil conditions. If area codes do not specify the slab reinforcement material, order 6x6 - 10/10 welded wire mesh.

A 6-mil polyethylene vapor barrier should be installed over the gravel before the slab is poured. This will help to forestall moisture problems later.

If you are preparing the footing trench yourself, make certain it extends below the frost line. The poured concrete or block foundation wall should be built up to extend 8" to 10" above grade level.

CONCRETE BLOCK FOUNDATION

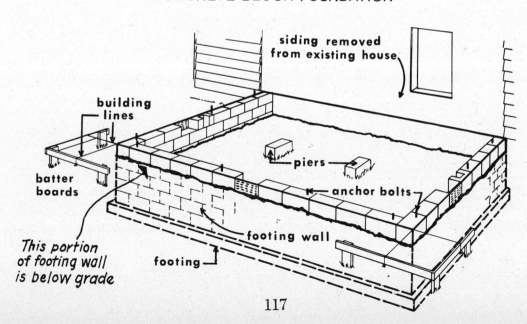

siding removed
from existing house

building
lines

batter
boards

piers

anchor bolts

footing wall

footing

This portion
of footing wall
is below grade

117

FRAMING ABOVE FOUNDATION

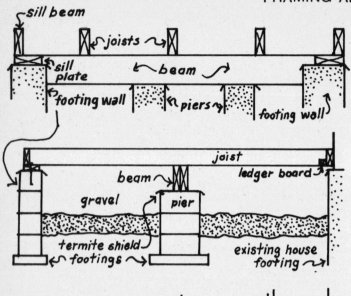

These section-thru views of floor framing show foundation, piers and floor framing from two directions:

1. Toward the house from the outer foundation wall.

2. From sidewall to sidewall.

If you have a 12' span or less, you may be able to eliminate the center supporting beam. For spans over 12', using the center pier and beam support would allow the use of smaller floor joists. Remember, you will want a solid, sag-free floor in your new room so don't skimp on the framing. The footing should be allowed to "cure" and settle for a few days before starting the floor framing.

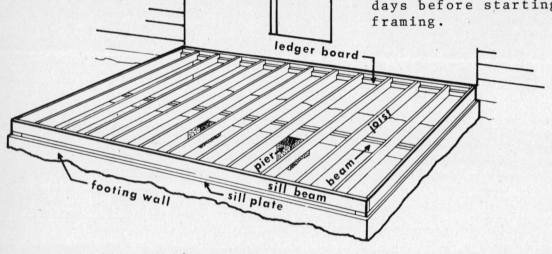

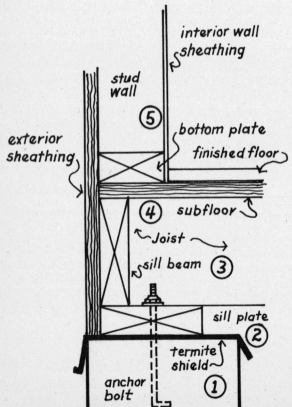

Perimeter anchor bolts are used to hold the sill plates in permanent position. They should be set every 3 to 4 ft. after the foundation is poured. Make sure 2 to 2 1/2" are exposed. Align them carefully.

This section drawing details the top of the footing wall, the protruding anchor bolts, sill plate, sill beam, the subfloor. The base plate for the stud wall is next, followed by vertical framing members. Note that all of these are set back the distance needed to allow the sheathing to be installed flush with the foundation wall.

After the concrete has "cured" for two to five days, depending upon humidity, the metal or plastic termite shield (1) and sill plate (2) are bolted in place. The sill beam (3) is positioned and toe-nailed to the sill plate.

118

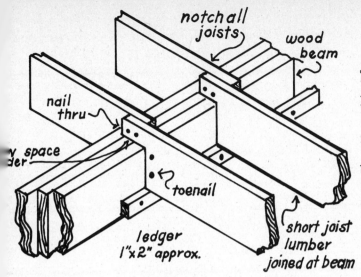

notch all joists

wood beam

nail thru

space [partial: y space / der]

toenail

ledger 1"x 2" approx.

short joist lumber joined at beam

The subfloor (4) is nailed to the joists and sill beam. The bottom plate (5) of the studwall is positioned and nailed through the sub-floor and into the sill beam.

Use the chart to determine the size of floor framing member. When a center beam is utilized, use the span between the sill beam and center beam.

FLOOR JOIST & RAFTER SIZING

50 POUNDS PER SQURE FOOT - LIVE LOAD			60 POUNDS PER SQUARE FOOT- LIVE LOAD		
JOIST SIZE	MAXIMUM SPAN ON 12" CENTERS	MAXIMUM SPAN ON 16" CENTERS	JOIST SIZE	MAXIMUM SPAN ON 12" CENTERS	MAXIMUM SPAN ON 16" CENTERS
2 X 6	8'·6" TO 10'·0"	7'·9" TO 9'·1"	2 X 6	8'·1" TO 9'·6"	7'·4" TO 8'·7"
2 X 8	11'·4" TO 13'·3"	10'·4" TO 12'·1"	2 X 8	10'·9" TO 12'·7"	9'·9" TO 11'·5"
2 X 10	14'·3" TO 16'·8"	13'·0" TO 15'·3"	2 X 10	13'·6" TO 15'·10"	12'·4" TO 14'·6"
2 X 12	17'·2" TO 20'·1"	15'·9" TO 18'·5"	2 X 12	16'·4" TO 19'·1"	14'·11" TO 17'·5"
2 X 14	20'·1" TO 23'·6"	18'·5" TO 21'·6"	2 X 14	19'·1" TO 22'·4"	17'·6" TO 20'·5"

If a center beam is to be used, use the span of beam to footing.

WALL FRAMING

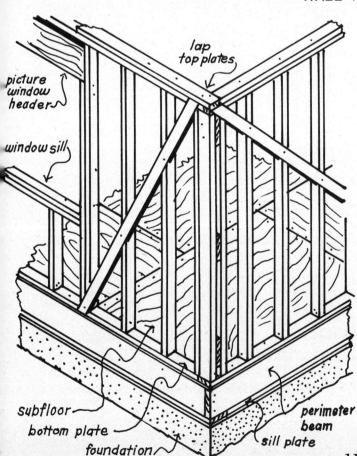

lap top plates

picture window header

window sill

subfloor

bottom plate

foundation

perimeter beam

sill plate

With floor joists installed and a subfloor nailed and/or glued in place, exterior framing can now be started. This is a good time to review the first portion of the book relating to wall construction and corners.

Walls can be prefabricated and raised into position. Temporary bracing is used to hold them in place while other wall sections are readied. Note in the illustration that the top member of the double top plate is overlapped at each corner. Nails are driven through both plates and into the built-up corner framing with 20d nails. The double top plate is required because the outer walls will be carrying the weight of the roof.

Corner bracing should be next installed. This usually requires 1x4 lumber set at an approximate 45 degree angle running from the bottom plate to the joint formed at the top

119

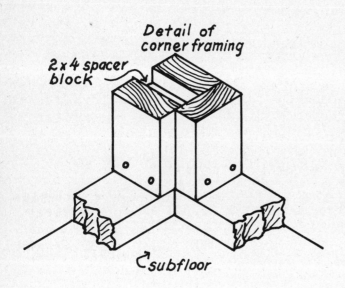

Detail of corner framing

2 x 4 spacer block

subfloor

plate and corner studs. It is "let-in", which merely means angle-notched studs along the path of the bracing so the brace itself is flush.

In some instances, a window or door may fall within the 45 degree line. The angle can be reduced, but the brace should fasten to at least three studs. When the angle is established, snap a chalk line to indicate both cuts for the notching. The top and bottom should be mitred. Drive two nails through the brace at each stud.

Corner bracing can be eliminated when 4x8 or longer sheets of exterior grade plywood or structural insulating board are installed vertically as the exterior sheathing. Joints should be staggered.

When plywood is used, the spacing of nails or staples around the perimeter should not exceed 6" ... 12" along intermediate studs. Insulating board requires more fasteners ... 3" spacing around perimeter and 6" for intermediate studs. The insulating board should be at least 1/2" thick.

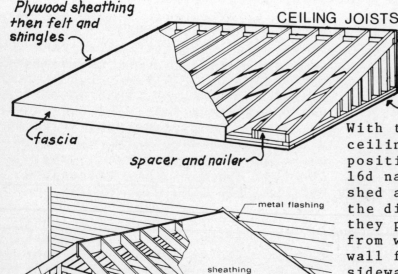

Plywood sheathing then felt and shingles

CEILING JOISTS

ledger

double 2x4 plate

fascia

spacer and nailer

metal flashing

sheathing

rafter

ceiling joists

wall top plate

With the walls plumbed and braced, ceiling joists are measured, cut, positioned and nailed in place with 16d nails. Look at the sketches of shed and gable roof framing; note the direction of run. In each case, they parallel the rafter run ... from wall top plate to the house wall for a shed; from sidewall to sidewall when a gable-type.

The joists of a shed roof are normally 2x8's set on 16" centers. The joists require support at the house wall so a header of the same dimensions as your joists is securely nailed to the existing house wall.

120

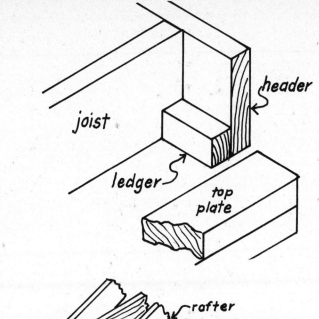

header

joist

ledger

top plate

The bottom edge is set at a height matching the top plate and is nailed through the sheathing and into the studs of the wall. A heavy string stretching from the top of the plate to the house wall can help fix the proper height. Use a level to check that the string is horizontal.

A 2x2 or 2x4 can then be nailed flush to the bottom edge of the header to form a ledger. Each ceiling joist is notched so it fits squarely on the ledger. Angle the nails down to gain more inherent strength.

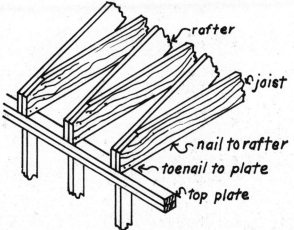

rafter

joist

nail to rafter

toenail to plate

top plate

The joists are toenailed on both sides into the plate and header. Later, the joists and rafters will be nailed together for added rigidity and strength.

When framing in joists for a gable roof, each end is toenailed to its top plate and, as explained for a shed roof, the rafters are ultimately nailed to the joists.

ROOF FRAMING

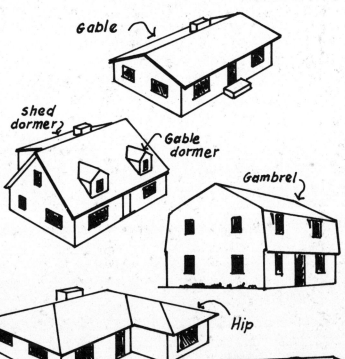

Gable

shed dormer

Gable dormer

Gambrel

Hip

mansard

As noted at the start, there are several basic roof styles plus variations on each. The principal shapes are flat, shed (a sloping flat), gable, hip, gambrel, mansard. Flat, shed and gable are the simpliest to erect ... the others require some experience and know-how with the framing square in order to properly measure and cut the various angles required. Therefore, the shed and gable are emphasized here.

Roof framing members make up their own vocabulary. Recognizing both the term and relationship in roof framing will help you in "reading" the illustrations.

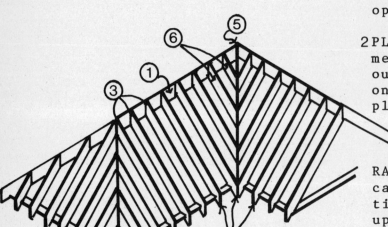

1 RIDGE - The highest horizontal framing member to which paired or opposite rafter ends are fastened.

2 PLATE - The horizontal supporting members of a wall. In framing, the outer end of the roof rafter rests on and is nailed to the double top plate.

RAFTERS - The sloping members which carry the roof load. Rafters are identified by various names, depending upon their location and function:

3 <u>Common</u> ... because all are of the same length as on shed or straight gable roof.

4 <u>Hip</u> ... these extend upward diagonally from an outside corner of the plate to one end of the main ridge. Each individual hip rafter forms a ridge where two adjacent surfaces of the roof meet.

5 <u>Valley</u> ... used where two roof surfaces meet. They extend from the intersection of two ridge boards downward to the intersection of two plates forming a corner.

6 <u>Jack</u> ... occurs in any roof which has either a hip or valley rafter. A jack rafter is, in effect, a common rafter with a shortened length created by its connecting point to a hip or valley rafter. A hip jack extends from a plate to a hip rafter; a valley jack extends from a ridge to a valley rafter.

SLOPE - The degree of rise from plate to ridge.

7 RISE - A vertical measurement that is always combined with another term "run,"

8 RUN - A horizontal measurement to describe a slope in exact numbers. Example: A roof might have a 6 inch rise (elevation) for each foot (horizontal) of run; therefore, 10 feet of run would result in 60 inches of rise ... or 5 feet.

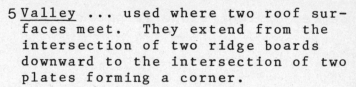

Notching detail

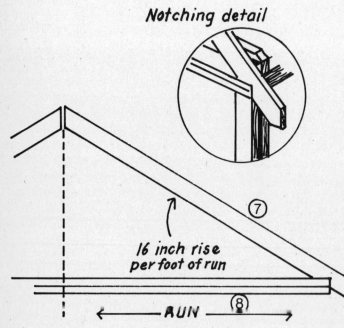

16 inch rise per foot of run

RUN

FRAMING SQUARE

raming square is like a slide rule
beyond comprehension until you try
When you find it actually works,
becomes a valuable project tool.

raming square is used for rafter
ming, stud spacing, rough framing
doors, windows, fireplaces and
ilar openings.

ood framing square is made of stain-
ss steel or other metal with a rust-
sistant plating such as copper, gal-
ized or nickel. It consists of a
DE 2" wide and 24" long; a TONGUE
" wide and 16" long. Numbers and
es are etched into the metal.

e FACE is identified by the stamp
the manufacturer's name. It is
ided into 8ths and 16ths. The back
s three gradations ... 10ths, 12ths
1 32nds. The tables for rafter fram-
are shown on the face. The HEEL is
e outside corner.

e degree of roof slope or pitch will
termine how much longer the rafter
ngth must be than the apparent hori-
ntal run. The chart cites several
mmon rafter lengths needed to accom-
date various pitches. Note that a
ed roof will require one rafter for
ch 16" o.c. while the gable will use
o ... one for each side to the ridge.

e illustrations show how the angle
cut is established for a flush eave.
ded length must be provided for any
erhang or cornice. Detailed instruc-
ons for all uses of the square are
cluded with the unit. Read them
refully and test each application
urself. You will be surprised how
ickly basic uses become clear.

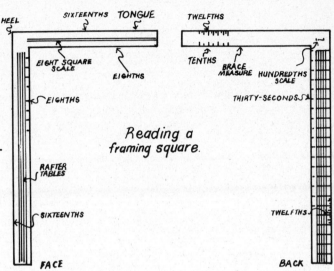

Reading a framing square.

MEASURING AND CUTTING RAFTERS

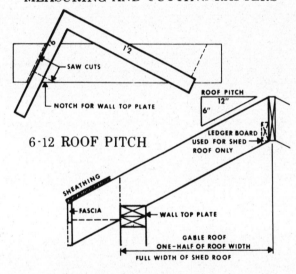

6-12 ROOF PITCH

5-12 ROOF PITCH

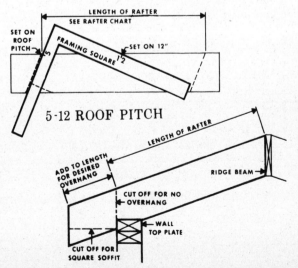

LENGTH OF RAFTERS CHART

Roof Width	Slope of Roof (Inches per Foot)				
	4"	6"	8"	10"	12"
10'	10'- 6"	11'- 3"	12'- 0"	13'- 0"	14'-1½"
12'	12'-7¼"	13'- 5"	14'- 5"	15'-7½"	17'- 0"
14'	14'- 9"	15'- 8"	16'-10"	18'-2½"	19'-10"

FLAT OR SHED ROOF

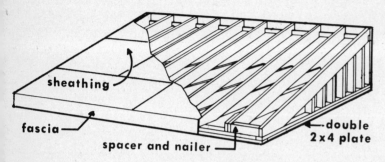

sheathing

fascia

spacer and nailer

double 2x4 plate

The flat roof is the least expensive to build and is certainly the easiest to construct. They are not common in the South where snow loads are not a weight factor to be contended with. Where winter snows are prevalent, the members have to be oversized in order to be strong enough to support the weight of snow loads ... sometimes two or more feet deep.

The nearest relation to the flat roof is the shed roof. The only difference is that one end is raised to provide a slope in one direction. A shed roof is merely one side of a gable roof. The pitch or slope can range from very slight to fairly steep.

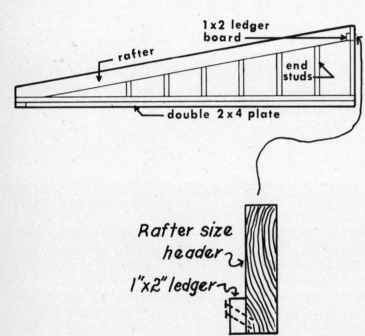

1x2 ledger board

rafter

end studs

double 2x4 plate

Rafter size header

1"x2" ledger

With the walls and ceiling joists installed, two decisions must be made ... the degree of slope and the amount of overhang, if any, to blend with the house. The construction is very much like that for ceiling joists. A header is nailed to the house wall at the appropriate height. The header should be the same dimension lumber used for the rafter ... usually 2x6.

A 1"x2" ledger is nailed flush to the bottom edge of the header. The rafters must be notched to fit over the ledger.

All rafters will be the same length. The angle to the top will be determined by the degree of slope. At the wall end, the rafter is cut so a flat surface rests on the top plate.

To make moving about easier and safer, lay several sheets of 1/2" or 5/8" plywood on to the ceiling joists to form a temporary floor.

Rafters are normally set on 16" centers. A stretched string will help position the first rafter. A 14 1/2" block can then be used to position each succeeding rafter. Toenail joists to the top plate and header.

GABLE ROOF

The gable roof has two sloping surfaces ... one on each side of the center line of the structure. The end walls follow the contour of the roof slope forming what is called a "gable end." This roof style is frequently combined with others, especially where a new roof will tie into the house roof. The pitch or slope of a gable roof can be slight to steep.

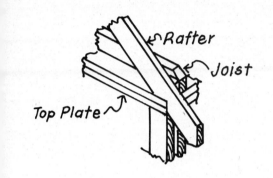

The top end of each common rafter is toenailed to the ridge, and the bottom end to the plate and adjacent ceiling joist.

When rafters run past the plate to create an overhang or cornice, they are notched so that approximately one-third of the rafter rests flat on the plate.

The build-up of a roof for asphalt shingles involves three materials ... 1) sheathing, 2) 15-20 lb. felt roofing paper, 3) shingles. Where wood shingles are used, horizontal boards are nailed to the rafters and the shingles are nailed to each row. No roofing paper is used.

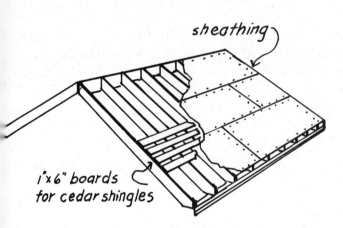

Enclosing a shed or regular gable roof where composition shingles will be installed is simple. Exterior grade 4x8 ft. plywood sheets are nailed in place with each succeeding joint staggered.

A 15-20 lb. roofing paper is nailed or stapled over the entire surface starting at the lower edges and working up. A 4" to 6" overlap is necessary to prevent wind-driven rain from backing up beneath the shingles and paper.

When working on a roof, wear rubber soled shoes; nail stout cross members between rafters for secure footing.

Where cedar shingles will be used, 1x6 inch boards are installed 4 inches apart. The spacing is simplified by having a 4 inch wide board to repeat the 4 inch gap. The

total of 10 inches allows for the
use of 16 inch cedar shingles with
a 6 inch overlap. The nailed rows
will be 10 inches apart. Use non-
rusting nails only.

Composition shingles have special
pre-formed shingles for enclosing
the ridge. Cedar shingles need a
6 inch width of felt paper stapled
over the top before these wood
shingles are nailed in place.

TRUSS SYSTEM

In certain instances a roof truss
might offer advantages. These are
complete roof and joist systems
which are prefabricated by a truss
manufacturer.

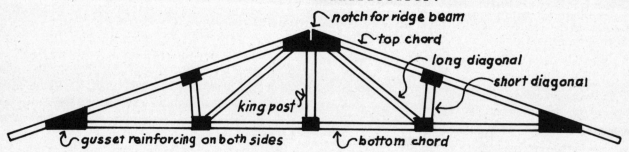

Several of the advantages are:

1. No complicated angle cuts to
figure because trusses are ready to
nail in position atop the exterior
sidewalls.

2. A truss system roof is self-
supporting; no interior bearing
walls are required ... divider
walls can be located anywhere desired and easily relocated at a
later date.

3. Trusses can be ordered in any
standard widths up to 34 ft. and in
any rise-to-run ratio needed to
match an existing roof line.

4. A prefabricated truss roof is
generally faster to install than
on-site construction; thereby reducing the time required to enclose
the roof.

There are different types of truss
construction ... a common one used,
king post, is illustrated.

EXTERIOR SHEATHING OF WALLS

Plywood or ructural insulating board

Gypsum Board

With framing completed, exterior sheathing should present no special problem. 4x8 sheets of insulating board or plywood should usually be installed vertically where no corner bracing has been added. This permits perimeter nailing. Review the information relating to corner bracing under Wall Construction for nail spacing.

Where corner bracing has been utilized, plywood can be installed horizontally. Note: When a shingle-type exterior will be used, threaded nails should be used when attaching plywood sheathing that is less than 1/2" thick. Allow 1/8" spacing along abutting edges and 1/16" spacing along abutting ends. Remember to stagger joists.

A 15 or 20 pound felt paper should be applied over the wall sheathing before applying shingles or siding. Overlap at least 4". Start from the bottom and work up. With this portion of the work completed, exterior doors and windows can now be installed.

SIDING AND TRIM

The exterior finish of the room addition can range from hardboard with batt strips, lapped metal or wood siding, composition or wood shingles to masonry (stucco), brick or stone facings. Each has its own requirements.

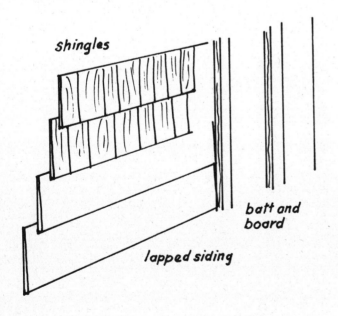

shingles

batt and board

lapped siding

Manufacturers of house finishes usually provide their own installation instructions which are specifically written for their particular product. Each new product brings forth a slight variation ... mostly to help the do-it-yourself family do the work. The siding should be selected well before construction starts; all pertinent information and instructions for installing should be reviewed carefully. Questions can usually be cleared up by the building materials supplier you will buy from.

A potential installation difficulty can often best be resolved with a snapshot of the particular problem area.

Plans and ideas

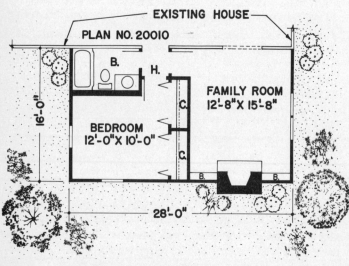

EXISTING HOUSE

PLAN NO. 20010

B.

H.

FAMILY ROOM
12'-8" X 15'-8"

16'-0"

BEDROOM
12'-0" X 10'-0"

C.

C.

B.

B.

28'-0"

TO ORDER ...
THIS IS PLAN NUMBER 20010
FAMILY ROOM - BEDROOM

As a service to readers interested in adding a room addition to their home, nine study plans for various types of construction are listed below. Included are garages, family rooms, bedrooms as well as multi-unit expansions. Each is identified with a number and title.

CONSTRUCTION PLANS showing elevations, framing requirements, section-thru drawings are available. Complete material listings by size and number of units needed are included.

To order a single set of plans, mail a check or money order for $25 plus $2.50 handling and mailing charge to H O W, Inc., P.O. Box 6216, Leawood, Kansas, 66206. Duplicates are available at $15 each when ordered at the same time. A set of four is $60 plus $4 handling and mailing charge. If a price change occurs after publication of this book, you will first be notified of the increase so you can elect to cancel or remit the difference before your order is shipped.

Also available is a selection of plans for vacation-type homes, including "A" Frames and Chalets. Selection of study plans similar to the ones below can be ordered for $3. Full CONSTRUCTION PLANS are available for each.

When ordering, make sure the plan number and the number of copies desired are clearly stated. Include your name, address and zip code on both order and envelope. Mail to:

H O W, Inc.
P.O. Box 6216
Leawood, Kansas 66206

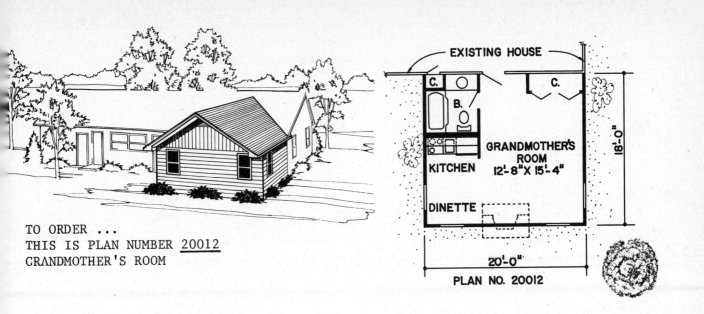

TO ORDER ...
THIS IS PLAN NUMBER <u>20012</u>
GRANDMOTHER'S ROOM

EXISTING HOUSE

C.   B.

KITCHEN

GRANDMOTHER'S ROOM
12'-8" X 15'-4"

C.

18'-0"

DINETTE

20'-0"

PLAN NO. 20012

TO ORDER ...
THIS IS PLAN NUMBER <u>20014</u>
GARAGE ADDITION - 2-CAR

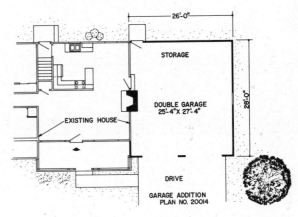

26'-0"

STORAGE

DOUBLE GARAGE
25'-4" X 27'-4"

28'-0"

EXISTING HOUSE

DRIVE

GARAGE ADDITION
PLAN NO. 20014

TO ORDER ...
THIS IS PLAN NUMBER <u>20016</u>
FAMILY ROOM - CARPORT

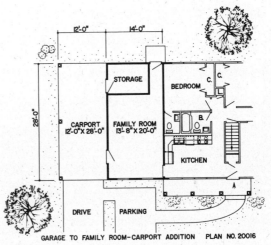

12'-0"   14'-0"

STORAGE

BEDROOM   C. C.

28'-0"

CARPORT
12'-0" X 28'-0"

FAMILY ROOM
13'-8" X 20'-0"

B.

KITCHEN

DRIVE   PARKING

GARAGE TO FAMILY ROOM-CARPORT ADDITION   PLAN NO. 20016

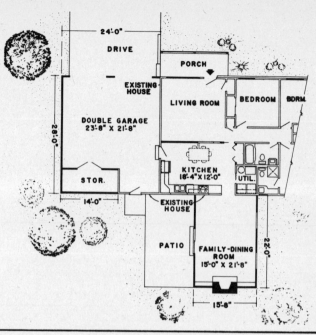

TO ORDER ...
THIS IS PLAN NUMBER <u>20018</u>
FAMILY ROOM – DOUBLE GARAGE

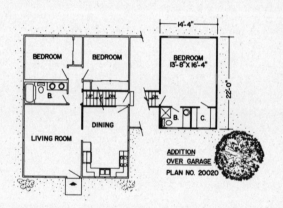

TO ORDER ...
THIS IS PLAN NUMBER <u>20020</u>
ADDITION OVER GARAGE

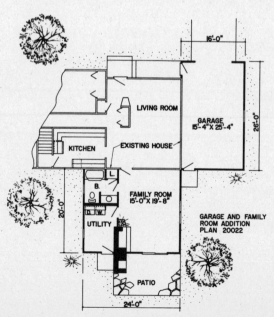

TO ORDER ...
THIS IS PLAN NUMBER <u>20022</u>
FAMILY ROOM AND GARAGE

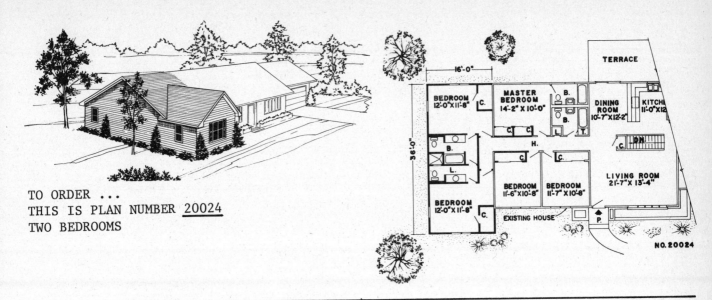

TO ORDER ...
THIS IS PLAN NUMBER <u>20024</u>
TWO BEDROOMS

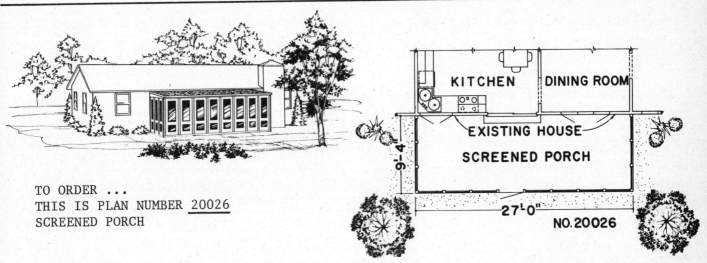

TO ORDER ...
THIS IS PLAN NUMBER <u>20026</u>
SCREENED PORCH

EITHER WAY ... YOU WILL SAVE!

Any room addition will require concrete footings and poured or concrete block foundation walls. These must be securely tied to the foundation of the existing house. Unless the owner has extensive experience plus some helping hands with know-how, the best bet may be to engage a remodeling contractor for at least part of the job. This might include all foundation work, rough-in framing including the roof. A further step would add all sheathing plus siding and roofing.

Time and ability will govern just how much you will choose to undertake yourself ... and how quickly you may want or need the addition finished. It should be remembered that the interior will still require a finished floor, ceiling and wall sheathing, all trim work and finish decor. Where permitted by code, electrical wiring for fixtures, outlets and switches might also be done by the owner.

It all represents time and work, but for the most part will prove enjoyable and self-rewarding. Of course, family members and unsuspecting friends can also be invited to participate.

To whatever degree you invest your time and labor, the savings can be substantial.

NOTES AND SKETCHES

NOTES AND SKETCHES

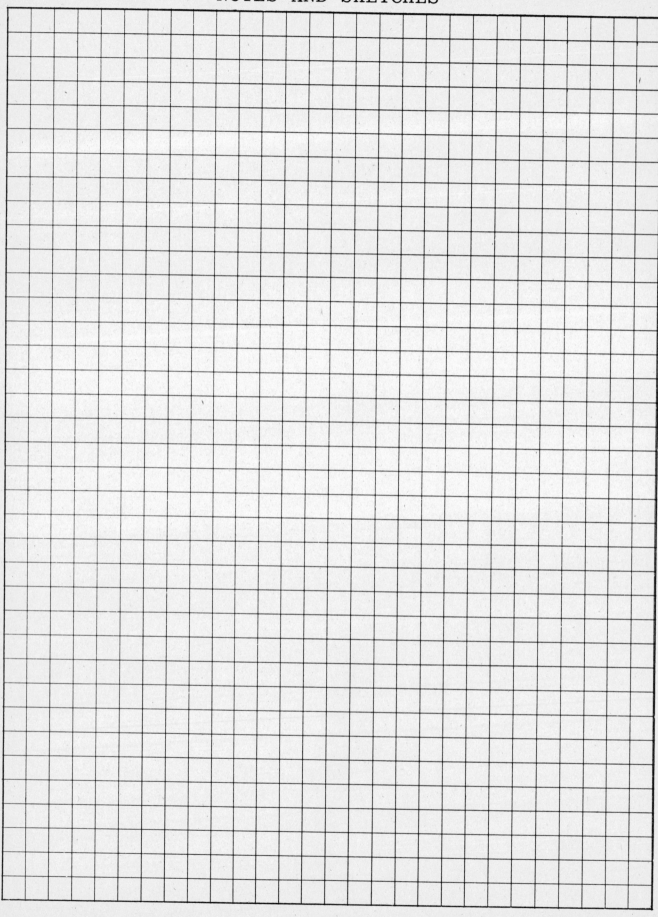

NOTES AND SKETCHES

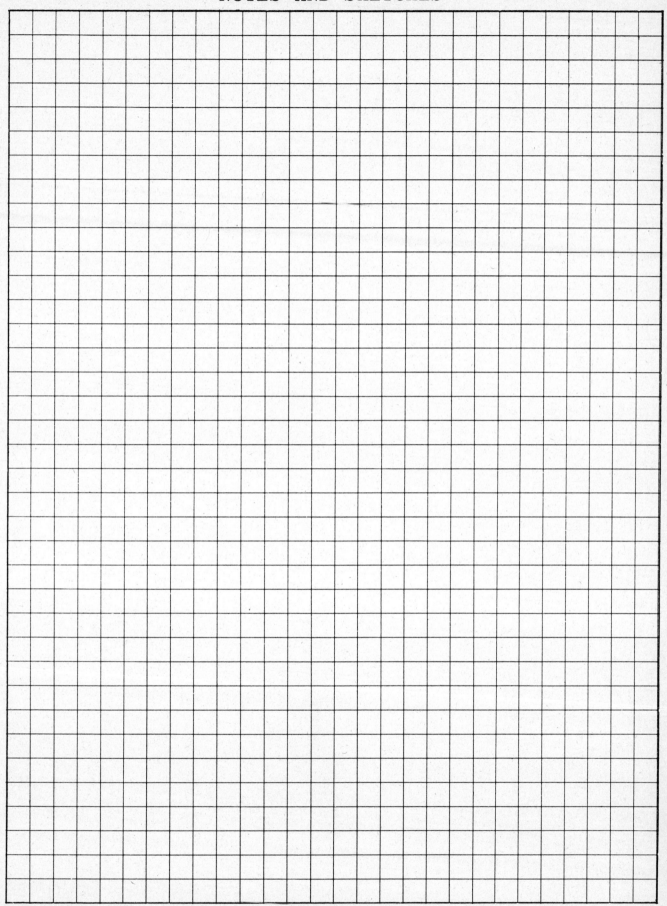

NOTES AND SKETCHES

NOTES AND SKETCHES

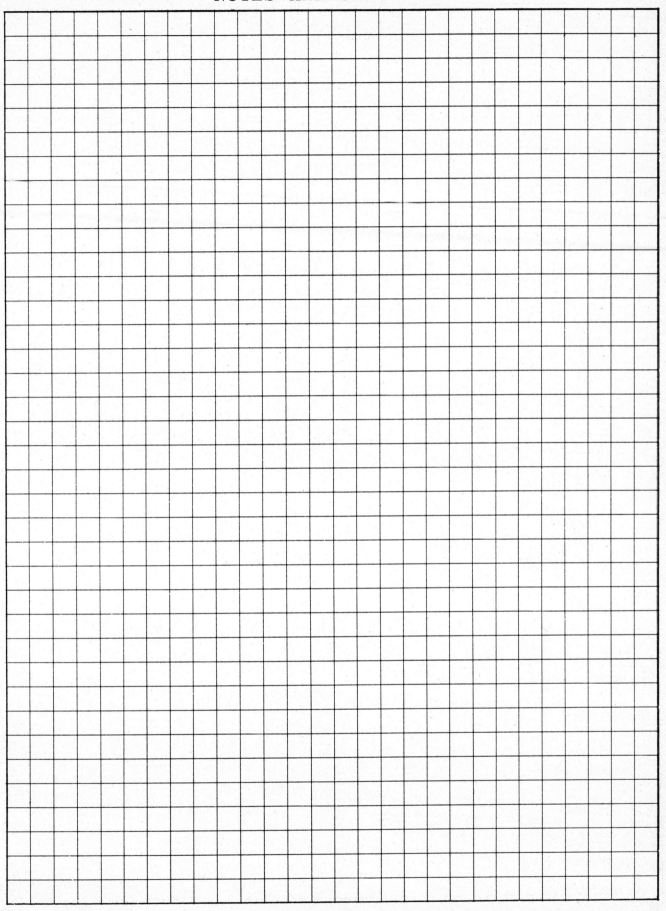

NOTES AND SKETCHES

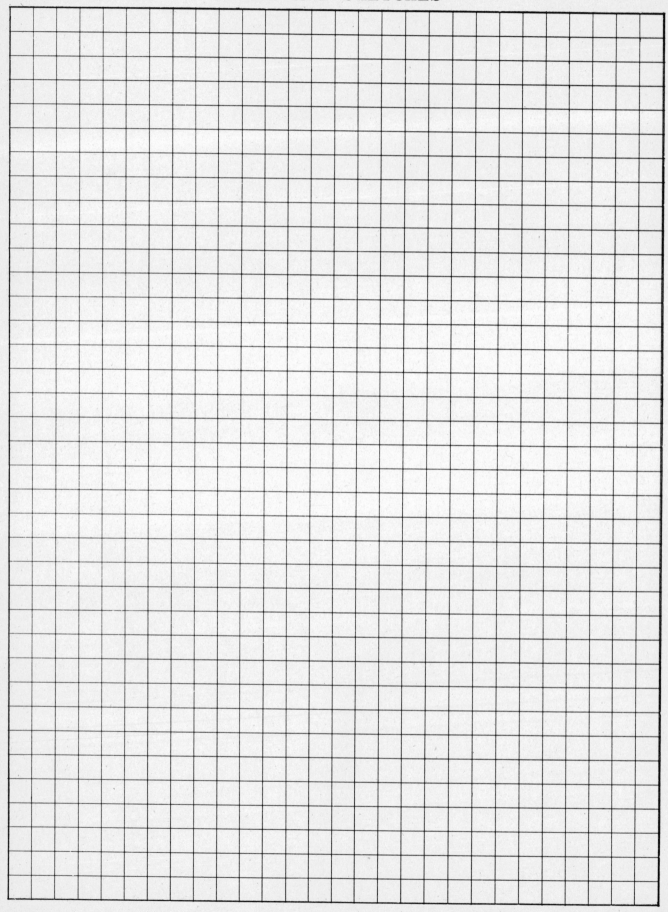

NOTES AND SKETCHES

NOTES AND SKETCHES

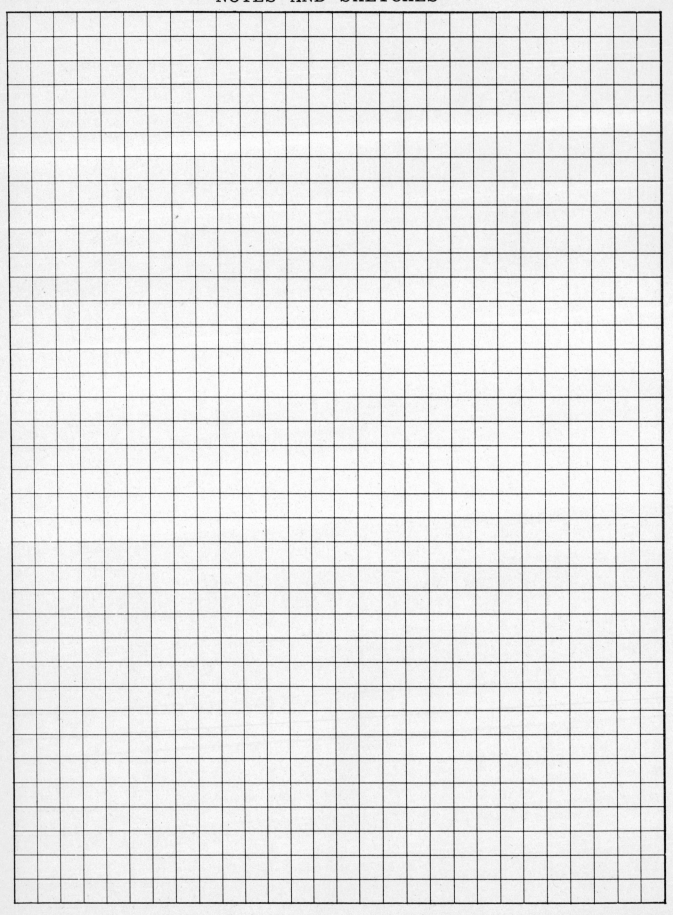

NOTES AND SKETCHES

NOTES AND SKETCHES

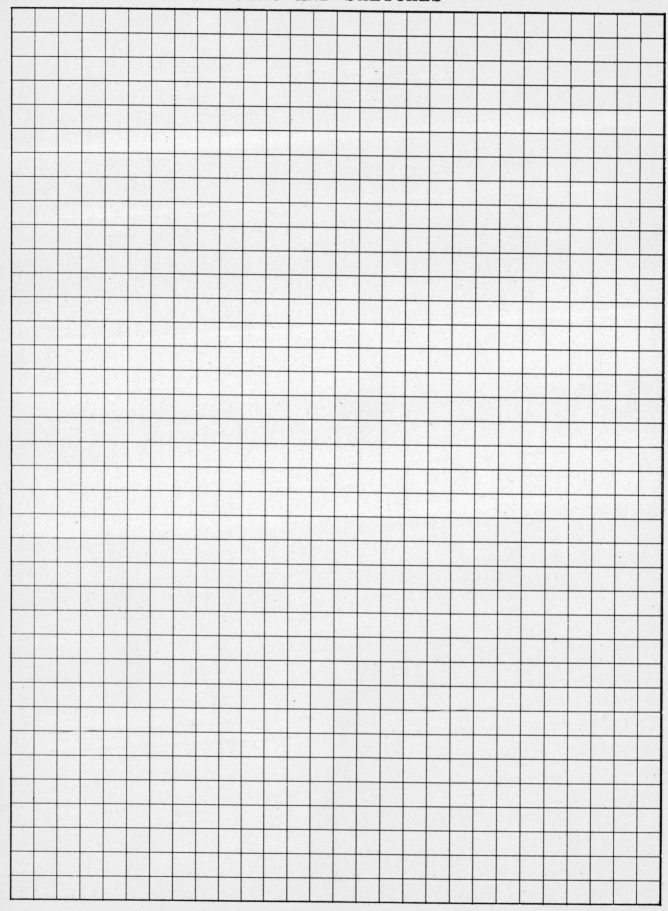

NOTES AND SKETCHES

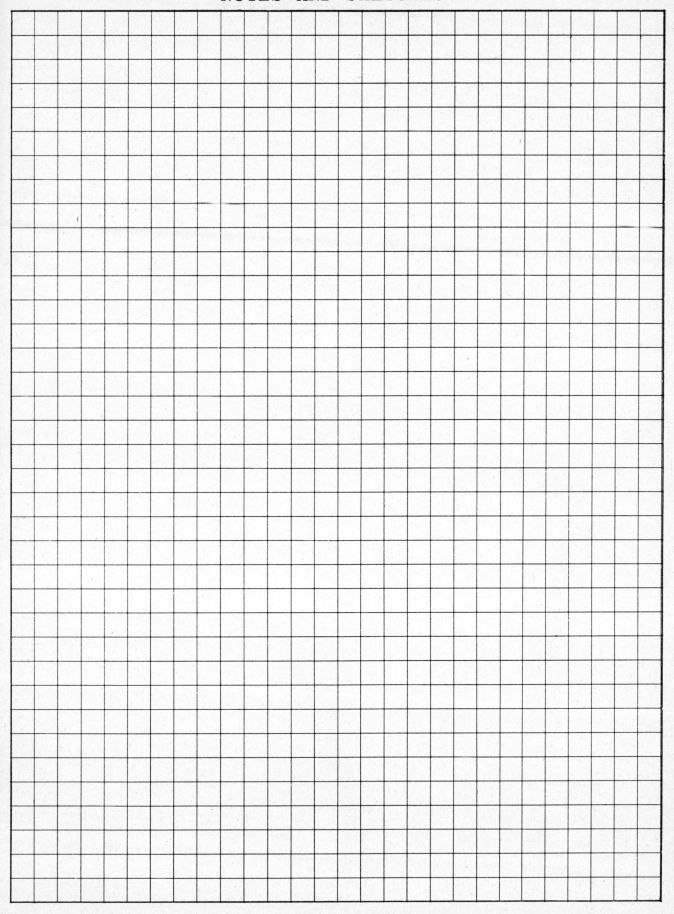

NOTES AND SKETCHES

NOTES AND SKETCHES

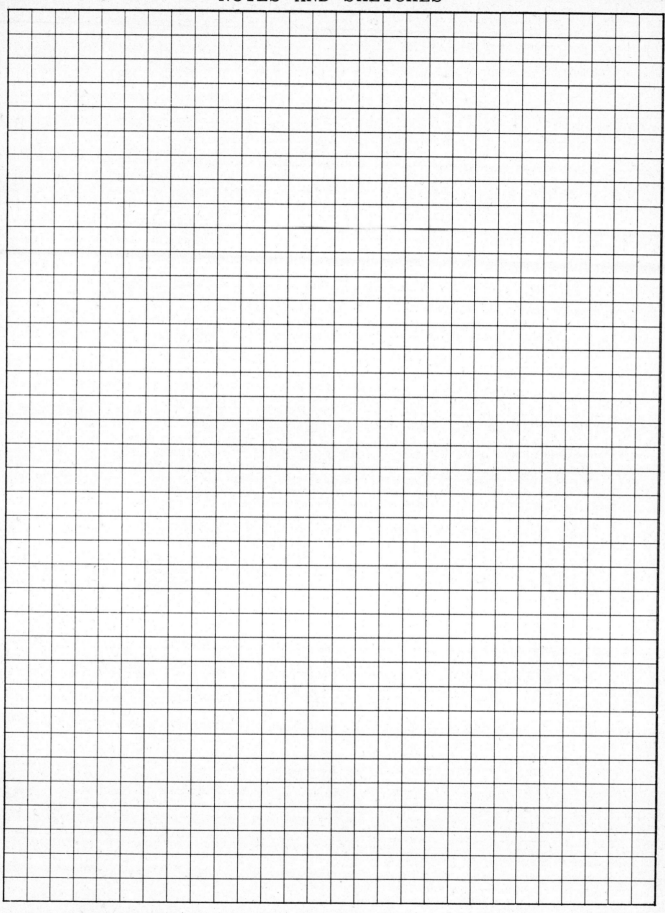